OPEN THE AKASHIC RECORDS FOR OTHER

STEP INTO YOUR POTENTIAL AS A READER,
CONNECT OTHER TO THE AKASHIC RECORDS,
DEEPEN YOUR CONNECTION WITH THE
UNIVERSAL MYSTERIES

CHERYL MARLENE

SOUL BRIGHT PRESS

CONNECTING

I'd love to connect with you!

Please join my newsletter and stay up to date with new books and special offers.

Follow this link:

https://www.cherylmarlene.com/newsletter

OPEN THE AKASHIC RECORDS FOR OTHER

Step into Your Potential as a Reader,
Connect Other to the Akashic Records, and
Deepen Your Connection with the Universal Mysteries

Library of Congress Control Number: 2019916207

eBook ISBN: 978-1-945868-33-7

Audio ISBN: 978-1-945868-35-1

Print ISBN: 978-1-945868-34-4

Large Print ISBN: 978-1-945868-36-8

CONTENTS

SECTION III
PROTOCOL FOR OPENING FOR NON-HUMAN ENERGY

SECTION IV
MOVING OUTSIDE THE WORKSHOP CIRCLE

SECTION I

LEARNING TO OPEN FOR OTHER

Welcome to the next step in your journey with the Akashic Records!

I'm glad you're here and excited that you've made this choice for yourself!

In Joy!
Cheryl

1

HOW TO BEGIN

This is a guidebook for you as you embark on a powerful journey of self-discovery. While it may seem contradictory, in practice, in the reality of your life, learning to work in the Akashic Records on behalf of Other is for you, this journey is yours.

This is a journey to explore, understand, and accept your worthiness as the amazing person you are.

Not a path of superiority. Not a path of altruistic self-surrender. Not a path of destroying ego. Not a path of separation.

Rather, a path of integration. A path of learning. A path into the depths of your being. A path for release of anything standing in your way.

In the pages which follow, and in the experience you will gather, are the encouragement and guidance to not only find your path of least resistance but also a path balanced beyond the arrogance of the ego and the smallness of self-rejection.

You learn to open the Akashic Records for Other not because you are better than Other or because you want to provide self-denying service. You learn to open the Akashic Records for Other because it is a powerful path of personal learning and experience of balance, authenticity, and awareness.

Begin with Your Akashic Records First

Self-trust and truth are requirements to fully embrace self-worthiness which is the primary journey of this book. Therefore, before beginning this journey, I highly recommend you complete my first book, *Open Your Akashic Records*. In opening the Akashic Records for yourself, you activate your awareness of the energy flow of your connection with the Akashic Records. This process of self-awareness helps you develop self-trust and opens you to receiving truth. This connection with trust and truth are vital and necessary to fully learn to access the Akashic Records on behalf of Other. Having personal experience opening your Akashic Records, you will have the necessary skills to take this much deeper step into the Akashic Records of Other.

What do I mean by Other?

Other doesn't mean just other people. Other means flows of energy *other* than your own. Mountains, businesses, buildings, animals, and more—any energetic flow which is not yours. In this book, your journey will focus first on people then you learn the protocol to open for non-human energy.

The Challenge Before You

While trust is the issue in your Records, now the challenge is your capacity, your ability. Are you worthy to stand witness for Other? Are you able to transmit the entire flow without causing harm? For this reason the journey is now about understanding your own worth. All of who you are and all of who you can become are the focus as you begin this journey. Along the way, there will be more lessons to help you release anything that no longer serves and whatever stands in your way of accessing the deep road of the Akashic Records as witness for Other.

New Agreements

Just as in opening your Akashic Records, you are asked to make agreements with the Akashic Records; there is a new set of Agreements which guide opening the Records for Other.

The most important agreement is to open only when asked by the Receiver and to never offer. This agreement, while of utmost importance, can cause difficulty for the student in practicing the new skill of opening for Other.

What is a Workshop Circle?

In direct workshop study with me, I create an energetic space of learning called the Workshop Circle. In this sacred space, I hold all students as they learn to open and work with the Akashic Records. When the student begins to open the Akashic Records for Other, the Workshop Circle provides connections with other students through a Reading Exchange so that a student's first opening for Other does not contravene the Agreements. Specifically, student practice is comprised of providing and receiving Akashic Record Readings with other students. Thus, the agreements are maintained from the beginning, and each student learns the importance of keeping the Agreements—especially to only open when asked and to never offer.

When presenting this learning process through a book, the teacher and student are at a remove. However, with the publication of this book, the Workshop Circle is a space maintained by the Akashic Records and is open to every reader with the intention of including you as a student. As you proceed through the learning process in this book, you will go through progressive stages of opening for Other with many practices suggested along the way.

To practice in a way which adheres with your Agreements, I will describe how you may create your own Reading Exchange, or you may choose to participate in the Reading Exchange which I maintain.

When you are ready to move beyond practice within the Workshop Circle, I ask you to do so with clear intention. The last lessons in this book describe the Clarity Protocol. This Protocol will help you be clear about how and when you open the Akashic Records for Other and will guide you to be in integrity with your Agreements.

How You Choose to Study is Up to You

Obviously, I can't control how you process the information and techniques described in this book. I can, however, extend best practices based on my years of experience – practices which maintain your integrity with yourself, with Other, and with the Akashic Records.

I know from over twenty years of experience with students and clients around the world that there will be those who listen to me and those who think they know better. Everything I suggest in these pages is geared toward what I know from this experience about what works and what doesn't. As I point out in my previous book, **Open Your**

Akashic Records, beginner's mind moves you into a space of learning. That is the best place to begin with this book as well.

Additional wisdom gained over the years taught me that practice done with friends and family is the least effective way to practice and learn to open the Akashic Records, particularly for Other. For this reason, I created a Reading Exchange which provides you a place to practice. Then, when you are ready, you can move outside the Workshop Circle with clarity and confidence, prepared to provide a quality Akashic Record Reading.

A lack of clarity about this on the teacher's part is detrimental to the student's success. Let me be clear:

When you provide a Reading to someone other than another person studying the method in this book (or associated workshop or Reading Exchange), you are now conducting an Akashic Record Reading outside the Workshop Circle.

PLEASE, complete the Clarity Protocol *first* before moving outside of the Workshop Circle and conducting an Akashic Record Reading. For your integrity and to support your deepest alignment with the Akashic Records, begin with the clear intention of you as an Akashic Record Reader obtained within the process of the Clarity Protocol. It's a simple, easy-to-complete process which will provide a firm, clear foundation for your efforts in the Akashic Records for Other.

Successful Completion

To ensure a thorough knowledge of, and later success in, opening the Akashic Records for Other, be sure you have done all of the following:

- Successful completion of *Open Your Akashic Records*, either book or workshop

- Read Section I of this book and complete the personal practices within the lessons regarding the Agreements, blessing, and process of opening for Other.
- Accept, sign, and date the Agreements for Opening the Akashic Records for Other (Lesson 10)
- Complete at least ten Biography Readings (Lesson 15)
- Complete the Readings with Mother Earth (Lesson 16)
- Create (and re-shape as needed) an Opening and Closing Dialogue (Lessons 19 & 21)
- Complete all lessons in Section II (Lessons 18-36), preferably within at least ten Reading Exchanges. If you don't have access to a Reading Exchange, then the lessons can be completed within your Akashic Records.
- Complete the lessons in Section III within the protocol for non-human energy.
- Complete the Clarity Protocol as directed in Section IV.

The learning process within this book is layered to open the deep road in the Akashic Records to you. You're here because of your serious intention, and I am here to support the depth of your intent. If you have questions or concerns, please visit my website (cherylmarlene.com) and either join one of my workshops, Master Class, or Reading Exchange – or use this email: connect@cherylmarlene.com

Because of the organization and depth of the material, this is a book to read start to finish. If you jump around, you will miss important points. The organization is intentionally multi-dimensional, and the unfolding is meant to support your own unfolding within this process of learning. Once complete, you will be able to return to whichever lessons call you to investigate again.

Provocative and intense, illuminating and freeing, may your journey provide you the depth you seek and the support you desire.

In Joy!

Cheryl

PS — I have a Reader's Packet ready for you on my website:

https://www.cherylmarlene.com/forother/

2

SELF-REVIEW

Before learning to work with Other, it's important to check in with yourself. Therefore, I always begin this entry into the Records for Other with a review of self.

The following questions help you review and open to the new work you are preparing to begin.

Gather what you need, open your Akashic Records, and ask these questions:

1. What is my truth today?
2. Find a passage or response in your Akashic Records Journal that, at the time, was very disappointing or for which you were unable to obtain a clear answer. Ask the same question now; make a request for more information, understanding, and clarification in your own Records.
3. Look for an example in your Akashic Records Journal which

resonated strongly. Focus on this passage and ask for further understanding or clarification.

4. Silence is a form and a non-form, meaning it is both substance and not substance. Ask for an example of something in your life with this dual characteristic and its effect or use in your life.

5. Is there anything for me to release or understand in order to learn to open the Akashic Records for Other?

3

WORTHINESS

Looking into the depths of self is scary. What if there is nothing there? What if what's there is no good, flawed, decrepit on all levels body, mind, heart, and soul?

The fear of being found out as a fraud, as less than, as valueless drives many to avoid learning, to deny self, to pull away beyond the attention of others and the flow of self-awareness. Avoiding the deep, humiliating pain of the possibility of being *less than* drives self to hide, diminish, and pretend.

At the same time, self is driven by an opposing fear. What if I am better than I can comfortably tolerate? Often the diminishment of self occurs to obscure the profound capacity of self.

The paradox of soul expression is fear of the opposing possibilities of being both too amazing and too broken.

This paradox is rooted in the primary concept of worthiness. On one side, I am not worthy. On the other side, my worthiness is beyond me. In either case, the choice is to keep self down, stepped away from true expression. Either way, the assessment is simple: I am not worthy. I do not measure up. I am less than and always will be. It is beyond me to accept that I am worthy.

Learning to open your Akashic Records provides a path to examine and embrace trust and to learn that trust leads to receiving truth. This prepares you for your next step: embracing your worth.

Here. Now. As you begin to learn to work in the Akashic Records for Other, your journey embarks on learning to accept the undeniable worth of you. Proof is not needed. Your value is intrinsic. Your worth exists, open and ready for you to acknowledge, claim, and declare.

Possibly contradictory, as you set out to learn to witness for Other. However, this is first a path for you to learn about you. Yes, you have flaws and challenges to uncover. They are different, however, from worth.

Worth is the acknowledgment and claiming of self as valuable, just as you are. No need for adjustments, improvements, or excisions.

To be able to witness for another requires a balance within the authenticity of self. If you are consumed with inner battle, then there is no energy for you to see beyond yourself. Compromised within, you will struggle reading for Other. You will question, and second-guess, and doubt what you receive—if you receive anything at all.

If you are not settled in your worth, then conducting a Reading will be difficult. You will question all you receive, how you transmit, and the value for Other.

When you peacefully accept your worth, the Reading flows through you without resistance, without judgment, without pressure to perform and prove your worth.

To feel worthy, doesn't require immediate improvement or upgrades. Simply, worth is acceptance of self just as you are, here, now. Worth is and needs no approval. Claiming your worth isn't about behaving perfectly. Learning and growing are part of life. Accepting the fundamental nature of self as worthy opens you to the deepest levels of growth and exploration.

Being right is another aspect of worthiness. Holding understanding of the Akashic Records in the static view will create the sense that connecting well with the Records is about being *right* in the delivery during a Reading. However, this is a false assumption.

Within the dynamic view of the Akashic Records, the flow of the Reading for Other occurs in the present moment following the intention of Other. There is no *right* answer, there is only your best effort to convey what is received in the moment.

Getting caught in the belief that you must deliver the *right* answer is dangerously deceptive. Believing you must deliver the *right* answer comes from the mistaken belief that you must prove your worth. The erroneous belief is: to be *right* proves worth. Given that worth is intrinsic and needs no proving, then being *right* is immaterial to transmitting a Reading within the Akashic Records for Other.

This will be discussed in further detail in a later lesson. Don't think of doing a *right* Reading or a *wrong* Reading. Instead, focus on a quality Reading; a Reading in which the Reader speaks truth, witnesses flow, and holds sacred space.

The determination of the effectiveness of a Reading is in the purview of the Receiver. The hard part to accept is that you can provide a quality Reading and the Receiver may not be pleased. This happens because the bias, on either side, is that only a positive experience is a *good* Reading. This overlooks the fact that sometimes what is in a person's highest expression is not pleasant or even understandable in the moment.

In my experience, some of the best Readings pushed at both me and the Receiver, upsetting and angering us both. But when I stepped back, listened, and opened my heart, I heard deeper truths and realized the negative response or emotion was released by the process of the Reading. If I, as the Reader, had been caught up in being *right*, especially in some provable way, then the Receiver and I would have missed the opportunity to see deeper and learn more.

As a Reader, how you hold yourself directly affects the Reading. If you are self-critical and inflexible, then the flow of the Reading will be affected and hinder the experience of the Receiver.

No matter the perspective, worthiness is the foundation of any Akashic Record Reading.

In accepting your worth, the need to measure up falls away. The worry of being special also fades because you are no longer concerned with outside validation. In the balance of self, authenticity is the guide and needs neither self-diminishment nor self-aggrandizement. Worth is the simple acceptance of self, just as you are.

In the quiet balance of self-worth, providing an Akashic Record Reading to another becomes a flow, freely extended without need to be praised. You receive and transmit the flow. Other receives, processes, and chooses for self within the discovery presented by the Akashic flow of soul energy.

Gather what you need, open your Akashic Records, and ask these questions:

1. Do I trust myself? If not, how not?
2. At the deepest levels of my being, how does my lack of self-worth express itself?
3. What immediate steps can I take to embrace the truth of my worthiness?
4. How is love connected to my sense of self-worth?
5. What can I do today to open my heart and live vulnerably, openly, and in complete trust?

4

STRUCTURE OF A READING

In early monastic traditions, the *lectio divina* was the reverential reading aloud of scripture or holy text. The Reader listened with body and mind, heart and soul, allowing the energetic spiritual resonance of the words to open an awareness of the presence of divinity within and without. The act of uttering sacred words with deeply meditative intention inspires connection with the Divine, with God, with All That Is.

In the same spirit, the Akashic Record Reading is an inspired reading aloud of an individual's divine soul story. The use of the word *reading* is purposeful in the context of the Akashic Records much in the same way as the *lectio divina* holds purpose: to connect to the deepest and broadest soul aspects of the person and recognize their deep affinity with All That Is.

When the Akashic Records are opened for a person, three elements join together to create the flow of the Reading:

Receiver: the person whose records are opened is the focus of the

Reading. An Akashic Record Reading is always driven by the intention of this person, the Receiver.

Reader: the person who opens the Akashic Records for the Receiver. The Reading is conducted and guided by the Akashic Records Reader within agreements and with a single focus, the Receiver.

Reading: the flow of knowing accessed, received, and transmitted by the Reader for the Receiver from the Receiver's Akashic Records.

An Akashic Record Reading always occurs in a unique moment of time. The Reader is who she is in the moment of opening. The Receiver is who he is in the moment. Neither will be the same people in a day, month, or year. Thus, the Reading presented and received in this moment is only possible in this moment and can never be repeated. This unique aspect fuels the resonance of the Reading and provides foundation for the sacred space of the Reading for both the Reader and the Receiver.

The Akashic Records may be accessed at many levels, across the entirety of the energy continuum, potential to form, spiritual to physical. With intention and with the support of Agreements, the Reader accesses the Receiver's Akashic Records at the Soul Point within Non-Physical Reality. Deep access at this level means that the Reading will be conducted from the soul's point of view and not limited to a physical perspective. In this sense, an Akashic Record Reading is a telling of the soul's story within the divine knowing of this moment, here, now.

The content of an Akashic Record Reading comes through the knowing of the Receiver's Akashic Records. In the context of the Reading, knowing has three aspects: knowledge, known, and knowing.

. . .

Knowledge

Knowledge encompasses in this moment what is known, unknown, and unknowable. Emerging from Non-Physical Reality, the knowledge of the Reading flows within this moment from the infinite and the eternal.

The Receiver will most likely be highly focused on the linear and the immediately practical. When someone has a burning desire to know, to have a question answered, or solve a dilemma, the strength of the motivation can narrow the focus. This reduced vision is part of the reason the Receiver is having difficulties finding solutions and has sought out a Reading.

The Reader, clear in the dynamic aspects of the Reading, holds a broad space to allow the Receiver to step beyond the known and receive from the unknown and the unknowable. A person comes to an Akashic Record Reading to learn what she doesn't know. The Reader, by opening the Akashic Records for her, opens a channel for the Receiver to access the entirety of knowledge relevant, in the moment, to whatever question or issue is raised. This openness allows the Receiver to move beyond limitation, and experience the Reading as a process of discovery, healing, and focused personal support. At its most profound levels, an Akashic Record Reading moves into the sacred space of knowing, healing, and spiritual practice.

Known

In a Reading, the known is of both Reader and Receiver. Each are who they are in the moment of the Reading, and each are experiencing a unique moment in their lives within the Reading.

The known has both physical and spiritual components which fuel the Reading. Both Reader and Receiver have practical, everyday awareness of what is needed to live fully within this physical arena.

Each also has access and support from the inherent spiritual transcendence of human life. They have had their own experiences filled with challenges and successes which fuels their known.

This aspect of known cannot entirely be eliminated from the flow of the Reading. The Reader's responsibility is to refrain from dumping his known on the Receiver, allowing the Receiver to move and receive beyond any limitations inherent in the known.

Knowing

Knowing is a gathering of what can be known in the moment and is the entire energetic flow of the Reading. In the beginning of the Reading, the Receiver is focused on receiving information to answer questions. This happens, in part, because most people think that information is the only benefit of an Akashic Record Reading. The Receiver is also wanting to answer a heart-felt urge to understand and feel clarity about life and the situation raised in the Reading.

The Reader, however, holds the broader understanding that the Reading is an energetic conduit from the soul which is transmitting knowing as a deep soul-level process of emerging awareness. In this awareness comes the ability to process—on all levels body, mind, heart and soul—anything which does not serve, following a path to release the unneeded confidently and completely. In other words, the Reader opens a much bigger door than is expected initially by the Receiver, a door to release, healing, transformation, and integration.

The combination of knowledge, known, and knowing moves the sacred space of the Reading to the edge between the unknown and the unknowable. At this edge, with expectation released, the unexpected moves forward to power clear vision and understanding which underlies the energetic motion of healing. Able to move beyond what is known, Reader creates the space for Receiver to discover more, beyond the habit of mind, and move into the abundance of heart and true soul balance.

The Reading lights the horizon. The Reader witnesses the motion. And the Receiver embraces new vision of self-discovery, self-truth, and self-trust.

A profound moment of love which gives full attention to the divine capacity of the Reading, the Reader, and the Receiver.

Bodies freed. Minds opened. Hearts balanced. Souls touched.

Gather what you need, open your Akashic Records, and ask these questions:

1. How do I embrace the energy of an Akashic Record Reader?
2. What can I do to best support the Receiver of an Akashic Record Reading I provide?
3. What is the truth today, for me, of the energetic flow of an Akashic Record Reading?

5

ROLE OF THE READER

Opening the Akashic Records for Other is a sacred trust and serious responsibility.

All that the Reader has learned in opening the Akashic Records for self forms the foundation to to provide a Reading to another.

The Reader needs the flexibility and openness of Beginner's Mind. Just as the Receiver wants to know beyond his known, the Reader must not be held back by the contents of his mind and needs to be open to new thoughts and unexpected possibilities. Only in this flexibility is the Reader able to ensure that the Reading provides the deepest and broadest to the Receiver. The strength and openness of a Reading reflects the capacity of the Reader to provide and the Receiver to open and receive.

The Reader must be present to the Receiver and to the Reading because the Reading flows always from the present moment and depends on the Reader to keep it anchored within the balanced center of this flow. In part, staying present is one of the primary reasons for the Reader to keep his eyes open when providing a Reading.

While the Reading is guided by the intention of the Receiver, the Reader also brings intention based on the Agreements made with the Records. The entire learning path to becoming an Akashic Record Reader and all the experience gained as a Reader informs intention each and every time a Reading is conducted.

Integrity as a Reader begins with the first steps taken to learn how to open and connect with the Akashic Records. The Reader's willingness to learn and release that which does not serve creates a path where self-honesty is honored and where honesty can be embraced by the Receiver. Like everything within a Reading, the Reader's ability to be in integrity creates opportunity for both Receiver and Reader to be vulnerable and willing to allow truth to move forward and shift the Receiver in view of her highest expression.

Most importantly, stepping forward as an Akashic Record Reader is a commitment to self. Through each Reading, the Reader learns to take loving care of self. The Reader learns to let go of personal baggage so that this heaviness is not projected into the Reading or onto the Receiver. However, this is not about condemning self as unworthy or about reaching a perfected state. Instead, this is about cultivating self-awareness and knowing that life is a journey of learning, releasing, and growing.

Becoming an Akashic Records Reader is not a destination. Instead embrace the journey as a process which supports the continual unfolding of self's highest expression. Whether it is the first Reading provided, or the 50th or the 100th — each time you, as a Reader, are a different person. Personal experience and growth are the elements of a Reader's path of self-discovery. One may only become the Reader of the 100th Reading by conducting the previous ninety-nine. There are no shortcuts. Nothing is gained waiting on the sidelines until some imagined form of perfection is attained. Be here, now. Allow your unfolding journey to begin now.

Gathering together beginner's mind, present moment, intention, and integrity, the Reader is ready to explore the three aspects of responsibility in providing an Akashic Record Reading. These responsibilities form the basis for the Agreements with the Akashic Records in conducting Readings for Other:

- Witness of the Flow
- Speaker of the Truth
- Holder of Sacred Space

Let's explore!

6

WITNESS

In opening the Akashic Records for Other, the worst transgression is to ignore the agreements and open someone's Records without being directly asked. On every level possible this is a serious violation of Other with profound consequences for the Reader who arrogantly proceeds.

Even when a request for a Reading is made, the Reader cannot be entirely clear of possible missteps. When opening for Other, the most thoughtless act is to dump your personal *stuff* into the reading, however well-intentioned. Your *stuff* includes your belief, expectation, opinion, judgment, thought, feeling, idea, or analysis. Your *stuff* in someone else's Reading is not appropriate for any reason. The Reading is for Other and follows their intention, their questions, their desire for release, understanding, and integration. Adding your two cents, your insight, your opinion is entirely inappropriate, disrespectful, and possibly harmful to both yourself and the Receiver.

I say this to provide context for what follows. My wish for you is that you follow the deeper road of the Akashic Records. To make this journey you need to understand both the depth and the inadvertent, yet avoidable, effects you may have when opening the Akashic Records for Other. I don't want you to feel you are flailing in the dark. Instead, I want you to feel confident within the gentle flame of light available to guide your way as you embark on this journey.

Within a Reading, the point of attention for the Reader is as witness.

The witness observes and does not intrude. The witness transmits but does not add or edit the transmission. The witness receives openly and conveys clearly. The witness holds sacred space as supportive foundation allowing Other to make their own choice. The witness is neither judge nor jury, withholding nothing, providing no opinion.

Intention of the Receiver initiates the flow of the reading. However, as witness, the Reader's attention illuminates the flow. As witness, your attention to subtle nuance expands the possibilities of the Reading for the Receiver. Your attention connects the known, the knowledge, and the knowing available within the flow of the reading. Without your attention, the intention of the Receiver will not be attended to or resolved. As witnesses, your job isn't to get the answer. Your role as Reader is as witness giving attention to the flow raised by the Receiver's question and transmitting as clearly and as succinctly as possible to the Receiver. Through this transmission, the answer will come to the Receiver.

Each Reading is a unique experience with powerful potential to shift and expand both Receiver and Reader. Both stand at the edge between the spiritual and the physical, between the static and the dynamic, between separation and unity. Each person is who they are in the moment with a unique combination of life experiences, challenges, lessons, and blessings.

As Reader you show up as you are, heart open, eyes and ears attentive, willing to witness the being and becoming of the amazing individual before you. You can and must separate yourself and your uniqueness from the experience of the Reading.

Being asked by the Receiver to provide a Reading is a true calling, one which is not to be ignored. Remember, what is being called forth is your ability to stand as clear witness to the flow of Other. As witness, your responsibility is not to answer but to transmit, not to judge but to hold space, trusting self that the truth of the Other will step forward and make itself known.

Gather what you need, open your Akashic Records, and ask these questions:

1. What are the positive qualities of a witness in the Akashic Records?
2. What are the challenges of a witness in the Akashic Records?
3. How do I step forward as a witness within the Akashic Records?
4. What is the connection between knowing and standing as witness in the Akashic Records?
5. What is the truth for me today about being a witness for Other in the Akashic Records?

7

SPEAKER OF TRUTH

As a Reader of the Akashic Records, your responsibility within any Reading you conduct is to receive and transmit as truthfully as possible.

As a Reader, you are a speaker of truth.

What is truth?

Often the perception of truth is one which is fixed—carved in stone—and thus, immutable. Within the static view, truth needs to be nailed down because in its fixed perspective, for any one question, there is only one truthful answer. Many come to a Reading to get truth, particularly in a provable form. The idea is that for a question asked, time, obtainable information, or experience should prove the validity of the response from the Records. In the static view, truth is an outside-of-self experience, validated by outside sources.

Within the dynamic view, motion in the Akashic Records begins with awareness of the present moment. Truth emerges in this moment as the infinite and eternal expression of your soul. The essence of soul is growth, learning, and expansion. At the soul level there is naught but shift, change, and emergence. In each moment, your soul expresses truth and, though there is always balance, where truth is, from moment to moment, also shifts and thus appears differently from moment to moment.

From the static point of view, this motion can be confusing, frustrating, and easily misunderstood as different because there is change from moment to moment.

However, from the dynamic perspective, the essence of the soul is immutable, dynamic truth. The static view of truth focuses on content; the dynamic focus is on the *how*, the expression, the infinite and eternal motion of soul as truth, in this moment. Instead of ascertaining truth through logical, rational evaluation, dynamic truth is the resonance of truth in this moment. In the dynamic view, truth is an experience, a process of attention to expression, in this moment, from the infinite and eternal aspects of soul. In the dynamic perspective, truth is essential expression of the boundlessness of your soul.

Thus, truth comes from the deepest sources of knowing, emerging always into the known from the unknown and unknowable. Each expression is different from all other moments. Each moment has its own truth expressing from soul essence. Truth shifts because the nature of who you are shifts. In the dynamic perspective, truth is always in motion because soul is always growing and expanding.

In an Akashic Record Reading, to be a speaker of truth is to give voice to this boundless expression for Other. As a Reader, you have a sacred responsibility to step past your own issues and give voice to the ineffable for whomever you provide a Reading. Your stuff is not the Receiver's truth—no matter how relevant it may appear to you.

In this dynamic view, the challenge is one of control. The static view of truth is about getting answers to manage or control experience in the future. Dynamically, truth comes when control is released, and intention is brought to the essence of soul expression in this moment.

For most people, this is an incredible shift in attention. To be a speaker of truth in the Akashic Records from this boundless perspective requires that you, too, make this shift, releasing whatever expectation, blame, fear, and judgment stand in the way of clarity.

You are not conducting the Reading to tell someone their truth. Instead, you are releasing control and stepping into the boundless flow of the Other, doing your best to give clear voice to whatever comes. Essentially, you open your mouth, trusting self to speak the flow of Other, for Other. There is no control in this motion and ultimately, with practice, as trust builds, there is no hesitation. You open the Records, step into the flow, and present yourself on behalf of the Receiver as speaker of truth.

Whether you are a beginner or experienced, as a Reader, doubt can creep in. Fear will also tread your path. Both will push you to question your capacity and your veracity. Just as when you learned to open your Akashic Records, doubt will make you question whether you are truly in the Records, whether you are actually receiving for the Receiver and not yourself, and whether your delivery of what you receive is truthful, relevant, or actual.

Fear will insinuate itself, making you question yourself and the process especially when you begin to think of possible scenarios of seeing yourself as wrong or incapable. In the Akashic Records for Other, you have the power to influence and affect the life of another. Speaker of Truth is a sacred responsibility requiring the highest expressions of integrity. As you learn and grow, integrity shifts within, opening new awareness and new capacity.

Just as with the experience of opening your Akashic Records, each time you open the Akashic Records for Other, you are a new and different person. Trust is your path in providing the Reading. Trust underlies each word and each phrase which emerges to be expressed for Other.

You will never know exactly which words will touch and expand the person before you. You do not and cannot anticipate because the motion in the Reading, which will galvanize release and powerful motion forward for Other, comes not from you but from the deep expression of soul essence emerging for Other through the energy flow of the Reading. As speaker of truth, your only mission is to witness and transmit as best you can. Your responsibility is not to anticipate or figure out what needs saying in any moment. To do so is to engage your brain ineffectively and open a channel for harm to emerge which can affect both the Receiver and yourself.

In learning to open your Akashic Records, you practiced and developed an awareness of how the Akashic Records feel and express. You are no stranger to this connection, and this awareness provides a beginning point for conducting a Reading for Other.

Thus, don't debate. Follow the process, say the blessing, and open the Akashic Records for Other. Respond with whatever moves forward from the questions and issues raised by Other. Allow the flow forward without debate, questioning, or withholding.

Theoretically you should be able to transmit a response even if you do not intellectually understand the question. What comes is what comes. Your job, in its most basic form, is to transmit. Your job as Reader does not require understanding.

The greatest challenge in conducting an Akashic Record Reading to Other is you—your friendliness, your care for Others, and your desire to be helpful. You want to assist, to make a difference for Others, to support Others in their journey.

However, let's be clear: you are not here learning to be of service to anyone. What you, as the Reader, receive from providing a Reading is different from what the Receiver gathers in the Reading.

The Receiver seeks a path of self-truth so that they may feel confident and empowered to make a choice about the next steps in life. They may also, within the flow of the Reading, find and respond to a motion of release and healing which allows both transformation and transmutation.

You conduct a Reading to transmit this energetic flow as witness, speaker of truth, and holder of sacred space. You are a conduit of motion. You are not the decider of motion. In this moment, you simply say what comes to be said. As a speaker of truth, you do not insert yourself; you witness and transmit regardless of your thought, feeling, opinion, doubt, or self-judgment. Truth in this moment is guide, and the Akashic Records of Other is always the source of this truth. Not you.

You conduct Akashic Record Readings because doing so provides great joy and personal insight. You provide because the conveyance of a Reading aligns with your truth. Each Reading is unique in time. Within each Reading provided, you will learn more about yourself and your life. While your ability to stand witness extends support and attention to Other, the support has an indirect influence for you.

Understanding this effect on the Receiver of the Akashic Record Readings you provide helps you maintain integrity and appropriate boundaries. This keeps your actions true and ensures you keep your "stuff" out of the Readings you conduct. Importantly, your clear boundaries are the most powerful support mechanism for Other. In this clarity, Other can open deeply to the motion which brought her to the Reading and presents an open, unburdened path to receive her clarity, and her most effective path for balance and healing.

Over time, what you receive from providing a Reading for Other is simply a path towards a deeper understanding of trust and truth, and an expansion in your sense of worthiness. This motion forward, within your sense of worthiness, is not because you are helping to effect change for Other. This sense comes because you trust yourself to simply say, in this moment, the truth emerging from the Akashic Records for the Receiver.

Each Reading is a unique moment. You are who you are in this moment as is each person for whom you will read. Both of you have experience, belief, and feeling which are glorious aspects of the Reading for each of you. Neither person will ever be the same again.

You can't take yourself out of the energy of the Reading. Yet, you can be diligent in your efforts to not insert yourself into the energy and expression of the Reading itself. Any and all effects of learning and healing for Other will be more than you imagine or devise, if you will yield yourself and allow the flow to come entirely from the Akashic Records of Other.

This is not to say that there won't be something for you in any Reading your conduct. There will be. However, you don't get to it through intentional effort. Instead, it will flow to you within the process of the Reading without your intention to control or affect outcome.

There is an art to an Akashic Record Reading which comes over time, through practice. Pay attention not only to the big motions but also to the nuance of shift—those tiny, almost imperceptible motions which the rational brain tends to dismiss as immaterial if only because they are not perceived as worthy of attention. Often in these tiny jewels of awareness emerges the deeper path of shift and change. What will initiate change is not, and should not be, determined by the Reader. Often the overlooked expressions will return later in the Reading to be brought forward into the consciousness of and for the Receiver.

In the beginning, this was one of my biggest challenges because I thought it was my responsibility to make the Reading *good*. I wanted people to like me and find value in the Readings I provided. Looking back, I see how I got not only in my way but in the way of those I worked with.

Now that I have stopped questioning myself and simply transmit, I am constantly in awe of how the *little* bits – the nuance of shift – can be so powerfully effective. I can't know what and when these little bits will be influential, but when what I provide has a profound impact, the whole rhythm of the Reading moves further down the deep road. The possibilities for knowing and healing literally jump forward exponentially, and the person before me has a physical response of release and awareness. In part, this is why I conduct one-hour Readings. Most folks need about 35 to 40 minutes for the release to build and express. Often it is at this time that someone will cry, letting go of whatever no longer serves the best of their being and becoming.

The art of providing an Akashic Record Reading also shows in how you say what needs to be said. When you are in someone's Akashic Records, the response from the Masters, Teachers, and Loved Ones is to be expressed using various nuances of feelings. If what you receive comes with laughter, then transmit with laughter. If what you receive comes with a sternness of voice, then transmit with that same sternness.

Over time you will learn that there are different phrases that can be said to temper whatever needs to be transmitted. This, again, is the art of learning how to conduct an Akashic Record Reading. Learning how to incorporate different forms of attention into how you provide a Reading will come with the time and practice you put in to learning how to conduct an Akashic Record Reading.

I find myself saying different things at different times because, as a human being, I am aware that sometimes a ramp is needed to allow people to access what is being presented to them. If what you are receiving in the Akashic Records seems to be difficult for someone to receive, then you can add a phrase to preface what you transmit. Statements like, "This may be difficult for you," or "this may be difficult to hear at first." This is not adding your opinion to the

Reading; instead, with care you are facilitating the Reading, extending opportunity to the Receiver to hear and receive.

Gather what you need, open your Akashic Records, and ask these questions:

1. What are the positive qualities of a speaker of truth in the Akashic Records?
2. What are the challenges to a speaker of truth in the Akashic Records?
3. What stands in my way to truth, in the present moment?
4. What makes me try to control?
5. What stands in my way to stepping forward as a speaker of the truth within the Akashic Records?
6. What will help me be able to step forward as a speaker of truth in the Akashic Records?
7. What is the truth for me today about being a speaker of truth for Other in the Akashic Records?

8

HOLDER OF SACRED SPACE

S pace is both time and location—an interval which exists between this and that.

Space as location is often defined as a container such as a room, a box, or the contents of my heart. Space is that which is enclosed. Space expresses in a static view as physical location and in a dynamic view as energetic expression. Space then is unlimited, multi-dimensional across body, mind, heart, and soul.

Space as time passes statically from past to present to future, creating a line of events connected by the person who experiences this trajectory. I live my life and can recognize which event preceded and which event followed. Linear time is expressed in this inner awareness.

However, I can also have another experience of time which moves along the multi-dimensional trajectory of the dynamic expression of space as location. Connected intrinsically with All That Is, awareness in this moment is not confined to the static nor the linear and reaches out into the infinite and eternal. Dynamically the sense of time feels as if time is either not moving or moving very slowly. Dynamic time can also feel as if action is occurring independently from the clock ticking. In these moments, your awareness of time is connected with the experience of dynamic motion. Within a Reading, dynamic time fuels an experience disconnected from awareness of the passage of time.

Space can also have both physical and spiritual attributes experienced both independently and in synchronization. Space as both time and location in its multi-dimensional aspects is an expression of the unity which emerges from the integration of that which is physical with that which is spiritual.

Sacred is, by definition, the acknowledgement and the dedication to the transcendence of All That Is. The holy, the divine, the ineffable, the boundlessness, the beyond, yet generating the unknowable—all of this is recognized in the sacred.

Sacred space emerges at the intersection between the multi-dimensional aspects of physical space and the acknowledgement of spiritual transcendence. When space moves beyond just the physical, then space enters the realm of the sacred.

Sacred space exists with time as eternal and location as infinite. Sacred space moves forward into experience when you are able to acknowledge transcendence and open your body, mind, heart, and soul to the infinite and eternal possibilities inherent in physical-spiritual integration.

As a Reader, you are holder of sacred space for Other. To hold sacred space is to stand witness and acknowledge the transcendent qualities inherent within the depth and breadth of the Akashic Records.

An Akashic Record Reading begins when the Receiver asks for a Reading, bringing forward request, question, a longing to access knowing. The Receiver wants to be held within full attention of her amazing being and becoming. The Receiver wants support to move forward, beyond limitation, beyond encumbrances. Often stuck, unable to access the dynamic, to see beyond limits of mind and expectation, the Receiver reaches out for new, uplifting, and empowering support. Caught in an acute need to know, Receiver has missed the path to personal knowing in the moment.

By allowing self to witness and speak truth, the Reader can provide a Reading within the clarity and deep connection of sacred space. By acknowledging the responsibility of the Reader, which is emphasized within sacred space, the Reading stands within the light of transcendence and the anchor of physical expression.

An Akashic Record Reading is not limited to the spiritual. The most profound awareness comes from within the unity of sacred and profane, holy and every day, transcendence and physical presence, here and now.

Both the process and blessing of opening for Other provide connective tethers within sacred space. Intention forms the connection and begins the flow. The attention of the Reader holds space for the Receiver to connect and experience the Reading within the depth and breadth of being and becoming.

As an Akashic Record Reader, you do not need to do anything to intentionally create sacred space. The process of opening the Akashic Records for Other has embedded within its energetic connections all that is needed for sacred space to be the foundation of the Reading. As Reader, embracing beginner's mind and present moment with intention and integrity are the conduits of sacred space within the Reading.

Your role as holder of sacred space asks you to follow the process, say the blessing, and open the Akashic Records for Other. As witness and speaker of truth, you hold sacred space within the Reading, creating a clear foundation for knowing, healing, and spiritual truth to emerge for the Receiver.

. . .

Gather what you need, open your Akashic Records, and ask these questions:

1. What are the positive qualities of a holder of sacred space in the Akashic Records?
2. What are the challenges of a holder of sacred space in the Akashic Records?
3. What stands in my way to stepping forward as a holder of sacred space within the Akashic Records?
4. What is the truth for me today about being a holder of sacred space for Other in the Akashic Records?

9

PENALTY

When I first learned to open the Akashic Records, I made agreements, just as you, which defined and structured how and when I would open the Akashic Records for Other. I asked my Akashic Records what the penalty would be for going against the agreements. The response I received remains true to this day.

Experiencing a physical result from breaking the agreements is highly unlikely. Lightning won't strike. Your tongue won't shrivel. You won't go blind or lose your hearing. Nothing like this will happen.

Instead, an energetic fog will settle over your body, mind, heart, and soul. This fog is what descends when you are not honest, when you break agreements, when you lie. Sometimes you may feel the fog, feel how it throws you out of balance. The fog can be dry and ash-like or it can be wet and viscous. Either way, the energy muddies intention, adds burden, and dampens the awareness of your heart.

To release the fog, you must be willing to look at the detriments, accept responsibility, and deal with the consequences of the broken agreement. This release process will disperse the energetic cloud. You will feel lighter, cleaner, released.

The major problem with the fog is that, if you have been out of integrity for any reason, you may not be aware of the fog and how it hangs on your heart. By continuing to ignore truth and agreements, lying creates an environment where justification or blame may push you to be less than honest again, and again, and again. Once you start down a road of broken promises, energetically the push is to keep with the lies, the denials, and the other ignored bits.

But, to release the fog, you must be willing to take care of yourself and do the hard work of acknowledging how and why you are out of integrity. This is a cleansing process aimed at blowing away the cloud and releasing self from an energetic space limited by the consequences of the transgression.

Only you will feel your dishonesty. Only you can ask for atonement for yourself and within yourself.

Know that, as your experience with the Akashic Records progresses, your sense of integrity will sharpen and be refined with experience. Where integrity is today, may not be where integrity was yesterday. You're dealing with a moving target.

Within your Akashic Records practice, the blessing and process serve to connect you with the Akashic Records where you are in this moment and not where you were yesterday. As integrity sharpens, defiance of Agreements will be less common and, if it occurs, will most likely be more easily identified and released.

Remember, please, that the worst effect for the Receiver is you dropping your *stuff* into another's Akashic Record Reading. Regardless of how certain you are of having the perfect solution or the best answer, see these as yours. Understand that yours are not the Receiver's. In a Reading, when the Reader confuses the flow of the Receiver's Akashic Records with personal response, the Reader is no longer conducting an Akashic Record Reading. Instead, the exchange is person to person and no longer between the Receiver and the Receiver's Akashic Records.

Very simply, a Reading for Other is not for you. Keep *you* out of the Reading for Other and the Reading will be as intended for the Receiver. This is how you will maintain your agreements with the Akashic Records, and it is the only path to providing a quality Akashic Record Reading.

10

AGREEMENTS

Just as with opening your Akashic Records, there are agreements to make with the Akashic Records and with me, as your teacher, to open the Akashic Records for Other at the deepest and broadest levels possible.

Please, seriously consider every aspect of the Agreements. Consider what you need to do to maintain integrity and follow the Agreements. Your efforts within the Akashic Records will be enhanced and stable the clearer you are and the more you understand. The following commentary is meant to help you understand the deeper flows, though it will take practice and experience to begin to align and follow the deep road. Be patient with yourself. Allow the experience to flow and find guidance in unexpected locations.

At the end of this lesson, you will find the Agreements without commentary. From the Reader's Packet, print a copy to sign and date. (www.cherylmarlene.com/forother/)

I acknowledge, within the scope of the Akashic Records, that Other includes any and all flows of energy which are not mine.

You are learning to work in the Akashic Records that are not yours. In this context, Other means any energy flow which is not you. This includes all energy, including but not limited to other people, buildings, animals, businesses, rivers, mountains—and much more.

Each and every time I open the Akashic Records for Other, I declare my intention to always do so as a Witness of the divine flow.

To open the Akashic Records within the role of the witness is to claim a path of profound understanding powered by the soul energy dynamics of the Akashic Records.

May the flow be through me as a spark of recognition of All That Is, expanding the Knowing for all whom I witness.

The intention of the Receiver begins and directs the flow of the Akashic Record Reading. It is the attention of the Reader, as witness in an Akashic Record Reading, which supports the flow so that the Receiver may shift and release within the energetic flow. The attention of the Reader, as witness, opens the possibility for the Receiver to receive the infinite knowing of her soul.

May I move within the support of Beginner's Mind, Present Moment, Intention, Integrity, and Sacred Space.

Just as in your Akashic Records, the process of a Reading for Other is guided by the five concepts of the spiritual journey. Each time you open for Other, you do so as a beginner, present to the moment, with clear intention as a Reader, providing at the highest level of integrity for you here and now. With all these concepts fully engaged, you have the capacity to witness the Reading within the sacred space of All That Is and within the Akashic Records for Other.

The Agreements are arranged to support the three primary responsibilities of an Akashic Record Reader: witness, speaker of truth, and holder of sacred space.

I. Let me be a Witness of the Divine Flow.

Opening the Akashic Records for Other connects you with the divine flow of soul expression. In this place, extending full attention, you are a witness.

1. I will open the Akashic Records for Other only when asked specifically to do so by Other. I will never offer.

This is the single most important concept to receive from these agreements:

Only when asked, never offer.

Everything flows from this understanding. It is vital to your ability to maintain the highest level of integrity within the Akashic Records.

These two statements form the ethical framework for providing an Akashic Record Reading for Other. They are deceptively simple, yet powerfully supportive in maintaining integrity, thereby ensuring a moral perspective when working in the Akashic Records. Please, stop and think about what is being asked of you. You are not assuming you know better or have some magic solution. You can tell someone you open the Akashic Record, but you can't offer, if you are not asked. You will hold your tongue, even when other healers offer. You understand the ethics of choice and responsibility. Here, now, you are agreeing to maintain this ethical stance quietly, firmly, consistently.

You must be asked to open someone's Akashic Records. *This is not higher self to higher self. This is not thinking you will do someone a favor. Only a direct request is acceptable. In my case, people book on my website—this is a request from them to me. Or a friend calls and asks me to open their Records. Again, a direct request. There are absolutely no exceptions to this agreement.* **You must be asked.**

Offering relieves the Receiver of responsibility and transfers the responsibility of another to you. The only person you are responsible for is you—NOT another. Again, there are no exceptions to this agreement. I know you will be sorely tried on this. At some point, you will be certain that just this once, you may offer your best friend, or your sister, or the guy sitting next to you at a workshop. And most likely, you will offer. Then, you will find that it doesn't go well, or the person is offended, or you can't open their Records. Most likely, you won't feel right because you know that you have gone against these Agreements. Stop, and don't do it again. Keep clear boundaries, and your practice in the Akashic Records will flourish as you find the deep road.

2. I will request the Other's full legal name and birthday, using this information to guide my reading for Other in the Akashic Records. In the absence of a full legal name, I will consult with my Akashic Records as to how to proceed.

To clearly identify the Receiver, you will ask for their full legal name and birthday before opening their Akashic Records. The full legal name is the name on a driver's license, passport, or other legal document. The full legal name is the name that someone uses in legal proceedings. This is not the maiden name for those who change their names upon marriage. This is not a nickname or a name from a guru unless these names are legally part of a full name.

The birthdate is secondary identification acquired to insure you are not opening for a person younger than eighteen years of age. Interestingly, providing this piece of information establishes the integrity of the Receiver. You don't really need this information to open someone's Records. The full legal name together with the birthday create an energetic connection to follow into the Akashic Records. Later, we will cover what to do in the absence of a full legal name.

3. Only Other's intention and questions will guide the Readings I provide; never my opinion, judgment, expectation, or question.

The expression of the Receiver's intention guides the Reading and is conveyed through questions and issues raised. Not for any reason: you do not insert yourself into another's Reading.

4. Let me be as the ocean in flow with All That Is, allowing the highest expression to emerge and be transmitted to Other, whatever this may be.

Think of standing on the beach observing the ocean flow toward you. There is an ebb and flow, a continual motion of in and out. When you open the Akashic Records for Other, similarly an ebb and flow moves through you, bringing awareness and response. To the best of your abilities, you transmit the motion of whatever emerges in flow. When you don't insert yourself, then the Receiver receives the entirety of the flow and may respond to the full expression of their soul, in this moment.

II. Let me be a Speaker of Truth, as an echo of the divine flow.

As a speaker of the truth, you echo the soul's deepest calling and knowing to

Other. No withholding or determining appropriateness or accuracy. No worry or questioning. Transmit all that is received, clearly and kindly.

1. I will not memorize the blessing.

Each time you open the Akashic Records for Other read your blessing out loud like the first time...every time. Keep the blessing on a card in your Akashic Records journal or on your tablet or phone away from prying eyes. While, after enough practice, you may remember the blessing, put no effort into memorization.

2. I will never reveal the content of an Akashic Record Reading for Other, unless I receive permission from Other. I will guarantee 100% confidentiality and will not reveal the content to a third party, unless required to do so by law or within the teacher-student context.

Disclosure of the content of an Akashic Record Reading is the sole responsibility of the Receiver. The Reader, as witness, may not disclose anything from a Reading without the full, conscious permission of the Receiver. This limit on disclosure also extends to not acknowledging for whom you read. Without permission, any disclosure is a break in confidentiality and out of integrity.

Unlike a therapist or other medical practitioner, as an Akashic Record Reader, you have no legal protections for maintaining confidentiality. Though highly unlikely, theoretically you may be required to disclose the content of a Reading through legal channels. These agreements allow this disclosure, though it will ultimately be up to you to decide whether the situation warrants disclosure without permission.

Additionally, if you engage with me as your teacher, disclosure to me directly or within the learning opportunities I provide is admissible without violating these agreements.

. . .

3. I will withhold nothing of the flow, except in issues of death or abuse.

In an Akashic Record Reading done at the soul level, time can be tricky and is most often a feeling which you learn to translate. Energetically, the end of a cycle and the end of physical life can feel remarkably similar. So similar that telling the difference can be difficult. Additionally, physical death can be a very challenging topic to discuss. Because of the discomfort and the ambiguity in discerning physical death, you are not required to respond about death if you feel uncomfortable. Hedge with a remark like, "Feels like the end of a cycle for you."

In over twenty years of Akashic Record Readings, I have only been asked about the time or circumstances of a person's death three times. I have also had the honor to witness death, or its imminent arrival, several times. In all cases, the person came to their own conclusion and were thankful that full awareness came from within rather than having the awareness forced on them. This is a tight rope which you will learn to navigate with practice and experience.

Abuse issues can also be tricky. I believe it best for a person to open to abuse on their own terms and in their own time. Pushing a person beyond their comfort level is not helpful and can be traumatizing. Most often the Akashic Records will give indication that something traumatic happened and will guide you in responding in a general way. This encourages the Receiver to open slowly to events and experience and helps the Reader convey a process of discovery which empowers the Receiver rather than undermines. Additionally, there are Readers with their own abuse experiences which might be triggered by a Reading. Thus, abuse needs to be a topic which is handled with caution, especially in the beginning. The level of healing required in either abuse or death is of advanced technique and skill in the Akashic Records and is beyond the scope of this book.

. . .

4. I will flow within all senses and find ways to convey the feelings, thoughts, words, pictures, and experiences that I receive on behalf of Other.

With more experience with the Akashic Records of Other, you will find that not every Reading has the same rhythm or pace, the same tone or voice. The Akashic Records of the Receiver is unique in perspective and expression. Additionally, each Reader has their own personal style and expression. With experience as a Reader, you will learn to reflect the ambience of a person's Records to them in the way you transmit what you receive on their behalf. With experience you will also learn to bring awareness to more than just the big motions, but also to the nuanced and the subtle. Experience will guide you in understanding that nothing is held back for the simple reason that you will never know exactly what the Receiver needs in response to intention. Remember, what you receive will come through all your senses. Or, you may just know the response without needing to process sensory response. Simply transmit the best you can, trusting yourself to do so in alignment with the highest expression of the Receiver.

5. I will use expressions of love, compassion, and consideration in my work with the Akashic Records and throughout all aspects of my life.

Always conduct a Reading with kindness. The art of providing an Akashic Record Reading is guided by respect, honor, and consideration for the path of Other, not by sugarcoating or dissembling. Conduct the Reading with compassion and love for the Receiver. There is no need to limit this effort to the Akashic Records and every reason to extend this same respect and kindness to everyone in your life.

III. Let me be a Holder of Sacred Space for Other, creating room for the presence of the One and the Many.

Acknowledging the transcendent motion of the Akashic Records connects Receiver and Reader within a flow where the many and the One can communicate and support. Holding this sacred space is the responsibility of the Reader.

1. I will only open the Akashic Records for individuals 18 years old or older.

Eighteen is regarded as the age of adulthood. While there are plenty of immature fifty-year-olds, the point is to work with adults and not toy with the energy of a child. The adult can give full, cognitive agreement when asking for a Reading. This age requirement also provides a boundary for the Reader in the face of pushy parents. Most questions parents have about their children can come from the parents' Akashic Records. You work with adults and adults only.

2. During an Akashic Record Reading for Other, I will be present and in good health, and will not consume alcohol, drugs, or other disrupting substances within twelve (12) hours of a Reading.

In the twelve hours before conducting a Reading, avoid whatever keeps you from being fully present. Perhaps it is a lack of sleep, a head cold, or one too many cocktails at dinner. Maybe it's too much caffeine, a sugar buzz, or allergies. My habit, even though I don't have an issue, is to avoid alcohol at dinner the night before working with clients. I also watch my diet, avoiding foods which leave me feeling heavy and foggy.

3. I agree to a twelve-month training period from this day and will not change the process or blessing during this period.

As in opening your Akashic Records, you need a firm foundation to trust yourself to open the Akashic Records for Other. To develop a firm foundation, stick to this process. Don't muddy your experience with other processes. Allow yourself to develop a strong connection with a singular focus on one process.

4. Before conducting Akashic Record Readings to other people outside the Workshop Circle, I will clearly state my intention to be an Akashic Record Reader by following the Clarity Protocol.

Everything flows within the Akashic Records through intention. As an Akashic Record Reader, intention begins with being clear about how and when you will conduct readings. The Clarity Protocol helps you step through a process to clearly define intention and define the parameters of doing Akashic Record Readings for Other.

5. I will not teach another until I have at least twelve months of experience opening the Akashic Records for Other.

Teaching someone to open the Akashic Records incurs responsibility. When you are a beginner, you do not have the foundation to support this responsibility. Proceed with caution. Remain in integrity. Be thoughtful about accepting responsibility for another, if at all.

6. An Akashic Record Reading lasts at least one hour, unless permission is granted from the Akashic Records for shorter periods.

To allow for the energetic shifts possible in a Reading, generally an Akashic Record Reading is one hour. Check with your Records during your Clarity Protocol about the length of the Reading you provide.

In the sacred trust granted to me by the Masters, Teachers and Loved Ones of the Akashic Records, I agree to continue to keep the

Agreements I made to open the Akashic Records for myself and I now freely make these agreements to open the Akashic Records for Other.

Just as stated, you are agreeing to continue the agreements made for your Records and willingly add these agreements for Other.

Agreements for

Opening the Akashic Records for Other

I acknowledge that within the scope of the Akashic Records that Other includes any and all flows of energy which are not mine. Each and every time I open the Akashic Records for Other, I declare my intention to always do so as a Witness of the divine flow. May the flow be through me as a spark of recognition of All That Is, expanding the Knowing for all whom I witness. May I move within the support of Beginner's Mind, Present Moment, Intention, Integrity, and Sacred Space.

I. Let me be a Witness of the Divine Flow.

1. I will open the Akashic Records for Other only when asked specifically to do so by Other. I will never offer.
2. I will request the Other's full legal name and birthday, using this information to guide my reading for Other in the Akashic Records. In the absence of a full legal name, I will consult with my Akashic Records as to how to proceed.
3. Only Other's intention and questions will guide the Readings I provide; never my own opinion, judgment, expectation, or question.

4. Let me be as the ocean in flow with All That Is, allowing the highest expression to emerge and be transmitted to Other, whatever this may be.

II. Let me be a Speaker of Truth as an echo of the divine flow.

1. I will not memorize the blessing.
2. will never reveal the content of an Akashic Record Reading for Other unless I receive permission from Other. I will guarantee 100% confidentiality and will not reveal the content to a third party unless required to do so by law or within the teacher-student context.
3. I will withhold nothing of the flow, except in issues of death or abuse.
4. I will flow within all senses and find ways to convey all feelings, thoughts, words, pictures, and experiences that I receive on behalf of Other.
5. I will use expressions of love, compassion, and consideration in my work with the Akashic Records and throughout all aspects of my life.

III. Let me be a Holder of Sacred Space for Other, creating room for the presence of the One and the Many.

1. I will only open the Akashic Records for individuals 18 years old or older.
2. During an Akashic Record Reading for Other, I will be present and in good health, and will not consume alcohol, drugs, or other disrupting substances within twelve (12) hours before a Reading.

3. I agree to a twelve-month training period from this day and will not change the opening process or blessing during this period.
4. Before conducting Akashic Record Readings for other people, I will clearly state my intention to be an Akashic Record Reader by following the *Clarity Protocol*.
5. I will not teach another until I have at least twelve months of experience opening the Akashic Records for Other.
6. An Akashic Record Reading lasts at least one hour, unless permission is granted from the Akashic Records for shorter periods.

In the sacred trust granted to me by the Masters, Teachers and Loved Ones of the Akashic Records, I agree to continue to keep the Agreements I made to open the Akashic Records for myself and I now freely make these agreements to open the Akashic Records for Other.

Signed:

Date:

11

VISUALIZATION

To open the Akashic Records for Other, you will use the same visualization, Balance between Heaven and Earth, with a shift. Instead of your Records, you will enter the Records for whomever you are providing a Reading. The blessing clearly identifies the Receiver.

Let's review the visualization — try to do so as a beginner, new to the process.

The first steps of the visualization create safe space for your journey. The next steps lead you and the Receiver from this physical world to the soul energy of divine knowing and the soul's origin where the Akashic Records are located.

Remember, this visualization also does something a bit unusual. Instead of specifically grounding or centering, balance is created between heaven and earth for both Reader and Receiver. It is very important to find this balance as you enter the Akashic Records of the Receiver. You do not need to worry about either grounding or centering first because the process of the visualization does this for you both, plus much more.

Additionally, there is very clear intention not to use chakras, meridians, or other energy centers for connection. Please avoid shifting the process to do this. You will miss the deeper connection if you insist on intentionally including these pathways.

Also, please note that the visualization has important elements which must remain part of your process. However, the nature of the elements may change over time. For example, a tree must always be part of the beginning. Yet, today the tree might be a maple tree and tomorrow a pine tree.

Please note that these are the key elements of the visualization which must always be part of your opening process when conducting a Reading:

1. Finding a tree and a safe, comfortable place.
2. Breathing in the energy of the earth through the soles of your feet.
3. Bringing in the energy of the heavens through the top of your head.
4. Feeling the center of your body wherever you feel this to be (because each person feels this differently, this is what **you** feel and isn't necessarily one specific point).
5. Feeling balanced between heaven and earth.
6. Following a path from center.
7. Finding an entryway at the end of the path.

In the next chapter, you will learn to use the visualization within the process of opening your Akashic Records for Other. Please review the visualization now.

Visualization:
Balance Between Heaven and Earth

Take a deep breath and release. Take another deep breath and release.

Begin by thinking of a tree and a safe, comfortable place. The tree can be real; the tree can be invented. The place can be real or invented. Put your tree in your safe, comfortable place adjusting either the tree or the place so that they go together and you feel safe and comfortable about both.

In your mind's eye, walk up to the tree. Feel its form, feel its beauty. Turn and stand with your back against the tree, your spine aligned with the trunk of the tree, your feet in amongst the roots and the earth at the base of the trunk, your head pointed up towards the top of the tree.

Now, feel your feet melt into the earth and the roots of the tree, and as you breathe in, feel the energy of the earth come up through your feet, up your legs and into the center of your body wherever you feel your center to be.

As you breathe in, bring the energy of the earth up through the soles of your feet, and into the center of your body.

Now, turn your attention to the top of your head, the top of the tree, and to the sky and stars and heavens above.

As you breathe out, bring the energy of the heavens down through the top of the tree, the top of your head, down into the center of your body wherever you feel the center to be. As you breathe out, bring down the energy of the heavens through the top of your head and into the center of your body.

As you breathe in, bring in the energy of the earth, and as you breathe out, bring in the energy of the heavens. As you breathe in and breathe out, feel heaven and earth meet at the center of your body.

As you breathe in and breathe out, feel yourself perfectly balanced between heaven and earth.

As you continue to breathe in and breathe out, focus at the center of your body where heaven and earth meet. See or feel a path extend from your center.

Follow this path wherever it leads you until you get to the end of the path. You will know the end because there will be some type of entryway. A door, a curtain, or a gate.

When you arrive at the entryway, open your eyes, say the blessing out loud, and open the Akashic Records.

12

BLESSING FOR OTHER

In opening your Akashic Records, you received a blessing to use. Now you receive a second blessing to use when you open the Akashic Records for Other. As with your first blessing, this blessing acknowledges the boundaries of the Reading and how connection with the Akashic Records will be made. In the next lesson, I explain how and when to use this blessing in the opening process. I recommend that you keep the blessing on a card or piece of paper inside your Akashic Records journal or in a private file on your phone or tablet.

Remember the blessing is always said out loud.

Opening:

I enter the realm of the Masters, Teachers, and Loved Ones of (State full legal name) and match our hearts and minds with theirs.

This first sentence begins the opening for Other by stating the Receiver's full legal name and by expressing clear intention for connection to be with the Masters, Teachers, and Loved Ones of the Receiver. As stated, the connection is through hearts and minds. Also notice that this first statement connects both Receiver and Reader with the Akashic Records of the Receiver.

Let us find through joy and wisdom the ability to open the universe and ourselves to greater possibility and deeper love.

A declaration of intention which specifies both how to receive (through joy and wisdom) and what to receive (possibility and love).

Eternal Source, fill our hearts with clarity and sacred power and show us <u>(State first name)</u>'s place of balance.

The first name may be a nickname or a shortened form of the first name.

Hear us now as we become one with the whole.

As an expression of the many, connection with the Masters, Teachers, and Loved Ones creates connection to the entirety of divine source. Working with the Akashic Records is always a connection of the one with The One through the many.

When we are complete, release us in love and admiration, keeping our energy raised.

Acknowledging the resonance with pure potential which occurs through soul level connection with the Akashic Records, this statement asks for this energetic effect to be maintained after closing. This resonance with pure potential will affect both Receiver and Reader during a Reading.

. . .

The Records are open.

Remember that since you are opening the Akashic Records for another, the Records opening are not yours.

Closing

In love and light, I thank our Masters, Teachers, and Loved Ones for their information and guidance.

The closing of the Akashic Records always begins by thanking the Master, Teachers, and Loved Ones for their connection and assistance.

Amen. Amen. Amen.

The purpose of saying amen is energetic. The repetition of this word allows you to move from the pure potential of the Akashic Records back into the physical space of your everyday life. Because as a Reader you are providing a Reading, the effect will also be felt on the Receiver of the Reading, and the amen brings them back as well.

The Records are closed.

Remember that the entire blessing is always said out loud so that not only you the Reader hear what you are saying, but more importantly, the Receiver of the reading hears and is included in the energy of the sacred space of the Reading.

Akashic Records Blessing for Other

Opening:

I enter the realm of the Masters, Teachers, and Loved Ones of **(State first name)'s** and match our hearts and minds with theirs. Let us find through joy and wisdom, the ability to open the universe and ourselves to greater possibility and deeper love. Eternal Source, fill our hearts with clarity and sacred power and show us **(State first name)'s** place of balance. Hear us now as we become one with the whole. When we are complete, release us in love and admiration, keeping our energy raised.

The Records are open.

Closing:

In love and light, I thank our Masters, Teachers, and Loved Ones for their information and guidance. Amen. Amen. Amen.

The Records are closed.

13

PROCESS

The biggest difference in opening the Akashic Records for Other is intention. Here the intention is NOT yours. The guiding intention comes from the Receiver of the Reading. Thus, the blessing specifies the intention of the Receiver. As the Reader, your intention is to support the Receiver.

Just as in your Akashic Records, the visualization and blessing join in service to the opening and closing process. As you begin to open the Akashic Records for Other, be reminded of the following:

Keep eyes open.

Your open eyes maintain the sacred space of the Reading for the Receiver. Your open eyes enable the Receiver to maintain connection with the energetic motion of the Reading. At times, you might use a soft focus and lightly close your eyes to see what you receive—but that's occasional, not all the time. This is true even when the Reader and Receiver are not together in the same location but are connected by phone or computer.

. . .

BREATHE!

When you get nervous, there is a tendency to hold your breath. Yet, in the Akashic Records, breath is what keeps the flow moving. I cannot over-stress the importance of breathing. While it's not necessary to use a special type of breath, you do need to inhale and exhale in a steady, regular rhythm. If it seems something is not flowing, not working, not something: BREATHE! Breath initiates and continues the energy flow of the Akashic Records.

Healthy and well for clarity and deeper connection.

If you are sick or feeling energetically depleted, this is not a good time to open the Akashic Records. Don't push or over-do. Open when your health is good and you are able to be clear and present.

Don't open while driving.

Operating any type of heavy machinery while opening the Records is physically taxing and dangerous. When the Records are open, the full attention needed while driving is diverted and not fully available. Stationary and fully present is best.

Process:
Opening the Akashic Records for Other

Before you begin, make sure you feel confident about the visualization and have the blessing for Other, and these steps of the process.

. . .

1. Ask for the full legal name and birthday of the Receiver. Ensure you know how to properly pronounce the name. Ask if you aren't certain.

Before you can open the Records for Other, you must have two pieces of personal information of the Receiver, namely the birthday and full legal name. As a reminder, the full legal name is the name on a driver's license or passport and is not a maiden or birth name if there have been legal changes. Out of consideration, be certain you know how to properly pronounce the full legal name.

2. Close your eyes.

The flow of the visualization is enhanced and more easily experienced by closing your eyes.

3. Balance between Heaven and Earth.

This is the visualization. Begin with your tree and safe, comfortable place and complete the visualization.

4. Extend your awareness along your path.

After finding balance between heaven and earth, feel a path extend from your center.

5. When you come to the end of the path at your entryway, open your eyes, and say the opening section of the blessing for Other out loud.

You are on the outside of the entryway; you have not yet gone through. Take a deep breath and feel yourself in this moment. Read the blessing for Other out loud, focusing on each word and thought, using the full legal name of the Receiver in the blessing.

6. Re-focus on your entryway, closing your eyes. Breathe deeply and feel yourself move through the entryway.

Remember this is the entryway to the Receiver's Akashic Records – not yours. It is very important that you go all the way through the entryway. Don't stop halfway. Go completely through the entryway.

7. Open your awareness to whatever you experience as you move through the entryway to whatever you find beyond the entryway.

This is the point which may be different from your Records. The entry may be the same or completely different. Know there is no expectation to meet. Whatever you find and experience is appropriate. Don't allow expectation to block clear and full entry. Don't debate with yourself about whether this is the Akashic Records. Assume whatever happens is the Akashic Records.

8. Say out loud "The Records are open." Feel them open if you haven't already.

It may take a few openings to settle into this process for Other. Not to worry! Enjoy the exploration and experience. Take a deep breath, release expectations, and trust yourself.

9. Open your eyes.

Remember: keep your eyes open while you are connected with the Akashic

Records for Other. This is very important at this stage and is, in part, the way the Receiver is connected to the energy space of the Reading.

10. Ask questions and respond as appropriate with all information.

Remember, you are not in your Akashic Records. Questions only come from the Receiver of the Reading. Your job is simply to convey what you receive as openly and accurately as possible.

11. When complete, say the closing section of the blessing out loud, "In love and light I thank our Masters, Teachers, and Loved Ones for their information and guidance. Amen. Amen. Amen."

As with your Akashic Records, you do not return to the entryway and the path, instead you use Amen. The first Amen brings you and the Receiver out of the Akashic Records. The second brings you both past the threshold between spiritual and physical, and the third returns you both to physical space.

12. Feel the entry close, and say out loud "The Records are closed."

Through clear intention, the Records close.

14

EXPERIENCE

As an Akashic Record Reader, I have had the privilege of witnessing many amazing events. In part, I hesitate to describe them because I don't want my words to be taken as either limits or requirements.

I have assisted many in releasing trauma by helping them to connect and release the erroneous notions created by the trauma, often standing witness as the person recovered memory or no longer denied events. I have witnessed the birth of a new soul and the release of the physical body. I have seen inside computer networks, worked with the Akashic council of a business, and supported folks to claim their career paths. I have witnessed various forms of physical challenges, the interference of past lives, and the origin of souls. Mother Earth has shown the vitality of our planet, calmed fears, and provided opportunities for deep, physical connection. The most uplifting has always come when I was able to rise above my personal expectations, assumptions, and definitions.

I extend the following support as you enter the deep road of the Akashic Records. Know that the universal mysteries are only accessible when you lay down what you expect to see and open to what you do not know in this moment. This way the Akashic Records have the space and opportunity to *respond from the depths of the infinite and the eternal, bringing to you the highest expression of being and becoming. Take a deep breath, and know you are ready now just as you are.*

Two Blessings

There are two blessings for opening the Akashic Records. The first opens your Akashic Records. The blessing in this book opens the Akashic Records for Other. Keep both blessings on separate index cards in your Akashic Record journal or on a phone or tablet.

Inner Work

Learning to open the Akashic Records for Other is as much about self as it is about learning to provide a Reading for Other in the Akashic Records. The lessons in this book are to help you explore the depth of your being and becoming. My hope is that you feel the safety, comfort, and support you need to move into greater self-understanding. I don't hold any ideas about exactly what that should be. As a teacher, my responsibility is to hold space for students not predict outcomes.

Flow Continues After Closing the Records

Just as in working with your Akashic Records, when providing a Reading to another, sometimes the flow continues to come after closing the Records. Think of a garden hose. When the water is turned on, the flow takes a moment to come out the end of the hose. In the same way, when the water is turned off, there is still water in the hose which needs to flow out.

After closing the Akashic Records, energy can continue to flow either in the form of knowing or a continuation of processing. This flow is something that hasn't yet entered the awareness of the Reader or the Receiver. If this happens, inform the Receiver.

Providing a Reading to Family and Friends

Providing an Akashic Record Reading for someone unknown is much easier than for family and friends. With an unknown person, personal want, desire, and intention are unknown and less likely to be disruptive for the Reader. With family and friends, their hopes and dreams are known to the Reader. This knowing can make objectivity difficult.

The lessons in this book open a path of experience in the Akashic Records for Other outside the circle of family and friends. This circle is the most likely source of practice. However, this circle will not provide the depth of practice most needed by the new Reader. Avoid providing a Reading to a friend or family member until you have some experience under your belt — ideally until you have made the clear intention to read outside the Workshop Circle, completed the Clarity Protocol, and have conducted several Readings for other people. Give yourself an opportunity to dig deep first.

Once you have completed the Clarity Protocol and have had experience beyond your family circle, you can begin to consider how to provide Readings to family and friends. I have found that there are some friends to whom I can provide a Reading without any issues for me or for them. While others, even with all of my experience, I refer to other Akashic Record Readers. My rule of thumb is to provide a first Reading with the caveat that I may need either to end the Reading early or not agree to a second one because we are too close.

Some family and friends will understand that the Akashic Record Reader is different from their friend. Some will not. Some will be able to maintain clear boundaries, and some will not. The Reader has the responsibility to be aware of and maintain appropriate boundaries.

The Agreements assist you with clarity especially when the person asking for a Reading is a close acquaintance.

As a professional providing Akashic Records Readings as part of my livelihood, I extend a friends and family rate. The first Reading is no charge, all subsequent Readings are at a reduced rate. I have a family rate because I am mindful of my value, and of my time and resources. It's very easy to let people close to you to take advantage. The only person who can keep you from giving away too much is you.

Scripts are not Necessary

Over the years, I have had students ask for scripts to use within a Reading for Other once the Records were opened. They wanted exact words to use for each step of the process and words to use to transmit whatever was received. I do not provide an exact script for several reasons.

Every Reading you conduct will occur in a unique moment in time for both Reader and Receiver. More than anything, the Reader needs to be confident to respond in the moment. A script will hold the Reading from the moment. The Reading will be rote, unable to truly respond to the intention of the Receiver in the moment.

A long list of requirements to be accomplished before opening the Akashic Records is onerous and unnecessary. In opening the Akashic Records for Other, simply be fully present, be clear about the process and your responsibilities as Reader, use the blessing, and request the Receiver's full legal name and birthday. That's it.

However, as you begin, especially with someone who you have never worked with before, the Receiver needs to know what to expect as much as that is possible. For example, the Receiver needs to know that the Reading is based on the questions that they ask. Often, they will want to know when to ask the questions or whether the questions are asked all at once or one at a time. In contrast, the Receiver doesn't usually want to know how the Akashic Records work in order to receive a Reading.

Instead of a script that I give you, it is better for you to think through, ahead of time, what you need to say to set the space for the Reading to occur within the unique flow of energy which holds the Reading. This consideration is not about creating the exact words to use very time. Instead the focus is to think of the content of what needs to be conveyed as you begin the Reading and as you close the Reading.

In later lessons you will develop both an opening and closing dialogue. The Opening Dialogue addresses what needs to be said before beginning whereas the Closing Dialogue addresses what needs to be said to close the Reading. Both dialogues help you identify what needs to be said at the beginning and completion of a Reading to establish the space of the Reading and guide the Receiver through the process of the Reading.

Dealing with Emotion

Almost every Receiver is nervous especially with the first Reading. There is no support in telling someone, "Don't be nervous." Better support comes in saying something like, "Feeling nervous is not unusual."

Whatever emotion is coming up within the person as the Reading begins is part of the Reading itself. The Reader does not get in the way of honest expression of emotion. Besides, advising against emotion is a form of judgment and will distance the Receiver. This is not a comforting way to begin a Reading. The Receiver wants compassion and attention. Dismissing emotion is not compassionate and creates space where the Receiver is perceived as less than.

.   .   .

A Reading Begins with the Receiver's Intention

An Akashic Record Reading does not begin when the Akashic Records are opened. Instead, a Reading begins in the first moment the Receiver thinks about asking for a Reading. When the Reader opens the Akashic Records for the Receiver, the Reader is providing the next step in a process which has already begun.

Not a Therapist

An Akashic Record Reader is not a therapist or a counselor. A Reader does not treat psychological trouble or heal mental issues. An Akashic Record Reader is not licensed to practice medicine, to heal, treat, or remedy challenges as a therapist or counselor might. A Reader does NOT fix the Receiver. At most, the Reader is a guide on the Receiver's spiritual journey providing spiritual support and insight. The Receiver heals self. The Reader witnesses the healing journey.

Questions One-by-One

An Akashic Record Reading proceeds through the questions raised by the Receiver. The Reading is more easily facilitated in taking questions one-by-one. Doing this keeps each question in the moment. The flow of the Reading will often shift the desired questions, bringing forward new ones and diminishing the need of others. Additionally, one-by-one helps the Reader maintain focus and relieves the Reader of the burden of remembering what was asked. If the Records want the questions all at once, they will make this clear.

Multiples

Other than study opportunities, work with one person at a time for the first year. An Akashic Record Reading generally is one Reader and one Receiver. This keeps boundaries clear, responsibilities straight forward, and confidentiality stable. Adding a second Receiver can complicate the flow of the Reading. The presence of another person who is "just there to listen" will influence and perhaps interfere with the flow of the Reading. As a Reader, be very clear about the intention of a second Receiver, insuring that you do not step into the middle of possible dysfunction.

It is possible to open two Akashic Records at the same time, though this is an advanced technique not covered in this book. It is also possible for two Readers to work together in the Records of one Receiver. Again, this is advanced technique.

Be Aware of You

In any Reading you conduct, be aware of how you show up and how you might influence the flow of the Reading. Pay attention to these elements:

- Your breath, your presence, your interaction, your impact.
- How you hold Sacred Space for possible transformation and integration.
- Your words and expressions as conduits that can allow energy to shift within if Other is ready.
- Your tact: be aware of the effect of your words
- Your ego: wanting to control the impact or direction of your words, demanding that Other be transformed and happy with the outcome, or trying to shape the Reading the way you see fit.
- Ability to concentrate and keep your energy balanced between heaven and earth.

Water Off a Duck

Let the energy of a Reading you provide flow away from you. I think of it like water off a duck. I don't absorb or take on the energy of the Receiver. The Reading is for them, not you. You have no obligation or requirement to take on their stuff. In fact, it is not healthy for you to do so.

Do not try to remember a person's Reading. I may recall significant details or large shifts, but I put no effort into remembering. First, I don't want to hold on to the "old" person in any way. Keep the path toward a new life clear and free. Also, if they return for another Reading, I want to deal with the person they are in the present moment and not whoever they might have been. Letting energy move on ensures you both are free and open to the present moment.

What's Next?

To open the Akashic Records of Other you now have all but one of the components you need. You need experience. Unlike opening for yourself, you will need to receive opportunities to open for Other.

Remember your Agreements include the requirement that you must be asked and that you never offer an Akashic Record Reading.

In the next section I describe three different paths to opening the Akashic Records for Other. Each path maintains your Agreements.

The last section of this book presents the Clarity Protocol to help you set your intention about how and when you will open the Akashic Records for Other outside the Workshop Circle.

SECTION II

READINGS WITHIN THE WORKSHOP CIRCLE

The Workshop Circle is the energetic space of learning within the Akashic Records which I support as a teacher. The Agreements with the Akashic Records are always maintained within the Workshop Circle.

As a new student, your practice in opening for Other must occur within the Workshop Circle. In the lessons which follow, all practices are done as directed within the energetic field of the Workshop Circle. Also as directed, you may join or create a Reading Exchange in which you practice providing and receiving Akashic Record Readings with other students.

When you are finished with practice or if you do not join or create a Reading Exchange, then you will complete the Clarity Protocol to establish your intention for providing Akashic Record Readings to those outside of the Workshop Circle.

After many years of teaching, I find that this process of clarity and intention provides the firm foundation you need to enter the deep road for Other.

Please do not underestimate the inherent integrity in this system of support for you.

15

BIOGRAPHY READINGS

*I*n learning the nuances and depth in opening the Akashic Records for Other, practice is a necessity. Every student I have worked with has remarked on the power of practice to enhance and expand their abilities within the Akashic Records. This is, in part, why I have created special opportunities for practice. I know both as a teacher and as a Reader the requirements for practice. This book, my workshops, and my interaction with reader and student are all geared toward providing the necessities for a firm foundation.

In working in the Akashic Records for Other, you as a new Reader need practice. However, within a book format providing this practice is challenging. AND the Akashic Records had a spectacular solution. Thus, as a reader of this book, your first experience of opening for Other will be in the form of what I call Biography Readings. In a special process, I have found volunteers who want to provide practice to those in need. As you read further, you will find Mother Earth has also volunteered. Plus, within a Reading Exchange I provide a format to find additional people so that all your practice will be in alignment with your Agreements and held within the Workshop Circle.

. . .

Because your practice with the Records for Other needs to stay within the parameters of your Agreements, I provide your first opening experience in the form of a Biography Reading.

Through the Akashic Records, I have found volunteers who have stepped forward to ask that their Akashic Records be opened by the readers of this book and the students in my workshops.

All Biography Readings are for deceased individuals no longer living on the earth.

As participants in the Workshop Circle, opening the Akashic Records for any of these volunteers is in alignment with your Agreements with the Akashic Records. Please note that this is not blanket permission to open for all deceased persons — you will learn this process in later books.

Short biographies are provided for each volunteer along with the person's full legal name, date and place of birth. The current age is the life age in which the person is asking his or her questions. Each volunteer has also provided questions that they would like asked within their Akashic Records for the time period specified.

To conduct a Biography Reading, follow this protocol:

1. Choose one of the volunteers from the following biographies.

2. Open the Akashic Records of the selected person using the process and the blessing for Other that you have just learned.

3. After opening the person's Records, say this biography statement out loud:

     On behalf of _____(full legal name)_____ may the response through me appear within the soul's awareness and the Akashic

Records of _____(first name)_____ as benefit, direction, and support.

---

4. Ask the questions listed within the biography, recording the responses you receive.

5. Before closing, repeat the biography statement, feeling the energy and response generated by the reading flow to the person through the Akashic Records.

6. Close the Akashic Records using the closing blessing and process.

For example, if you choose Matilda Sweeney, first open Matilda's Akashic Records. Insert her full legal name and first name in the biography statement. The questions you ask are hers as listed. In closing, repeat the biography statement, then close her Records.

Please note that the biography statements are presented as received through the Akashic Records. Dates and the names of geographical locations use the information presented. Thus, location names may not be the ones in use at the time. Additionally, not all questions are requested at end of life. Some are asked from a specified point and are identified as "Currently xx years old." This means that the questions are asked when the person was xx years old.

For practice, please conduct at least ten Biography Readings.

Matilda Sweeney

Chambermaid, born November 10, 1715 in York, England. Currently 23 years old with no family.

This is a lifetime of service for me to learn about the human condition. This is my first incarnation on Earth in the last 500 years. I am barely five feet tall, wearing a light blue dress with white apron and cap (covering my light brown hair.)

1. What are the lessons of humanity here, in England, in the early 1700s?
2. What are the struggles of the soul which cause one person to enslave another?
3. Why, especially in this time period, are women generally disregarded?
4. Why did my soul bring me here, now?
5. What lesson am I learning which can help you?

James Sweeney

Born August 3, 1701. Married Matilda when she was 26 years old.

I am a blacksmith, and I am now 56 years old and have had a very good life with Matilda and our four children, all sons except one. My sons have learned my trade, and we are part of the forces working toward a family place here in the Americas. I am excited, freely participate and have these questions:

1. In life on Earth, how do I maintain a sense of balance and connection?
2. Please talk a bit about developing a positive and supportive relationship with one's spouse.
3. What is the purpose of being a parent? Is it the same for all who become parents?
4. What legacy can I pass to my children?
5. What happens to the soul after death?

Consuela Villenova

Born 1901 in Madrid, Spain, currently 36 years old.

I work for the great lady in the household. My job is laundress and hearth sweep. During the day, I move from the dark room of the wash tubs to outside for drying. I must clean the linens of the household weekly. Every day is a different room. During dinner I sweep the hearths in the house, re-building fires. My only break is Sunday Mass. I have done this work since I was five years old, learning from my mother. These are my questions:

1. How can I find gratitude for this lifetime?
2. What are the effects of lead on the body?
3. What will this lifetime help my soul learn?
4. Where will I journey after this lifetime?

Al-Said

Born 715 CE, somewhere on the Arabian Peninsula currently, 45 years old.

I raise horses and other livestock for the men in my tribe. I am known for the strength, endurance, and sure-footedness of my animals. I have been granted a wonderful wife and several children who made their way to adulthood. I have these questions:

1. How are the sun and moon related?
2. What are the sands of time?
3. How do I know if I have lived a good life?
4. What can I do to support my wife?
5. How can I improve my connection with God?
6. What is my affinity with horses?

Sophia Newton

Born November 3, 1918 in Ireland, currently 42 years old.

I moved to England when I was 18 years old. I am now 42 years old, married and have no living children. My children died when they were four and five years old. My life has been filled with much death and disappointment. I spend hours in the cathedral praying and asking for guidance. As a result, my work has been reduced. My husband is very angry with me all the time, yelling insults and telling me I am worthless because he believes the deaths of our children are my fault. I should have known to do better and instead failed.

1. Am I worthless?
2. How can I become a better person?
3. Should I leave my husband? Where do I go?
4. What is the purpose of my life?
5. Why did my children die?

Joseph Langdon

Born December 13, 1832 in London, England, currently 42 years old.

Married to Elizabeth and have a daughter, Lizzie, and a son, Joseph. No other family. In my asking, I am 42 years old. I was an orphan raised in a monastery, educated there and given a sum of money to begin my way in the world. I made my way through law school and set up my practice in the town of Derbyshire.

I want to focus my learning about the potential of soul during physical manifestation.

I am 5 and half feet tall, 30 stone, brown hair and eyes. In many lives I have worked with the Akashic Records. We are fellow travelers. My questions:

1. What can I do to support my daughter in finding her soul's deepest expression?
2. What is the deepest learning for me in this life?
3. How do the experiences of this life contribute to the entirety of my soul?
4. What was the purpose of being an orphan in this life?
5. How do I navigate the rigid belief structures of physical life to experience life at the deepest levels?

Cha Kahn

Born about 700 CE in the Mongolian Highlands, currently 40 years old.

I am the leader of my tribe and have failed to be good to my people. Every day I look to satisfy myself with food and wine. I gamble with my chiefs and bed whoever I please. One night, another tribe killed me in my sleep along with most of my chiefs. Hanging over the tent site, I see my people celebrate their liberation from me. For the first time, I am aware of my horrible treatment of these people entrusted to me by my father. I feel my failure and their disappointment. I made life hard for them and can see that they had no choice but to eliminate the source of their pain. I will watch over them as guardian so that they may live in peace and prosperity. I have these questions for my soul's growth and understanding.

1. Why didn't I understand my failure before dying?
2. How can I release judgment on myself for my failure?
3. How does the concept "blindness of the soul" apply to me in this life?

4. In the perspective of my soul, what was the purpose of this life?

5. What are the lessons for me to learn?

John Ashwood

Born May 10, 1983 in Yonkers, New York, currently 26 years old.

I am a white male, age 26 years. I am a lawyer and a New York boy. I am seeking the meaning of life. I was newly graduated and was making a lot of money after being very poor, barely able to make ends meet. I purchased a "fast" car, married young, had one son. I had a hard time focusing on what was really important in my life and got mixed up in the fast lane. I forgot my humble upbringing and lost myself. I wish to participate to help younger souls integrate, focus on what is important in life, and learn the soul's lessons. I want to share what I missed for others to find their truth. I'm a nice guy but with a bit of a chip on my shoulder—that just makes me who I am. I died in a car wreck, probably my fault by driving too fast and under the influence of drugs. I have these questions:

1. What is the meaning of life?
2. What can I/we share to bring people to a wholeness of spirit that is currently missing in today's world?
3. What could I have done to be a better father, husband, person?

Mary Belle Ainsley

Birthdate: August 12, 1883 in Dorset, England, currently 43 years old.

I am English. I am a white female, age 43 years, and 5'3" tall, now living in Mansfield, England. I am a wife and mother. I have soft mousey brown hair and wish it was a bit thicker. I have been married 23 years to a man who drinks too much. He is usually in his "cups." My marriage was part of an arrangement. I am not much to look at, not a real beauty as some would say. But I have intelligence and character. I see through things, call a spade a spade, so to speak. Nothing much passes by that I don't see or discern. My man is not so much in love with me as to have me do for him. Our marriage was partly arranged by family. He needed a wife and I needed a husband. I have 3 children, now grown, and I will be a grandmother soon. My questions are about women and the right of a woman. I am intelligent, fully capable of running a household and keeping track of money and the wise spending of it (right down to the tinniest penny) or what money the husband does not spend on drink. There are some of us who are mightily capable of doing a better job managing than their husbands. Sometimes I search for a bit of autonomy so I can be my true self, but it is sometimes illusive. I have these questions:

1. Why can't women who are married own property in their own right? Why does everything go through him when he is less capable?
2. How does a woman find inner happiness when she is working from dawn to dusk with little or no regard from her husband?
3. For females, I would like to know why things are different now versus my lifetime from which I speak?
4. How does one deal with the frustration of being "put in one's place" constantly by society?

Abigail Adams

Birthdate: November 11, 1744 in Weymouth, Massachusetts, Female, currently 43 years old.

I am known as a president's wife, the First Lady of this lovely young country that has so much potential. I champion women's rights every chance I get. According to our Bible, we are all made in the likeness of God. This means both man and woman. We are different but equal. We are helpmates, just as capable as a man but with different abilities which should be recognized and honored. I am a great equalizer. I admit I have the uncanny ability to make a person feel at home around me, especially men. I use my abilities unfailingly in this way to promote prosperity, understanding, camaraderie, and a feeling of kinship with those political cronies who would rather use power and influence over others for their own gain. I wish to work for freedom and prosperity for this country and its peoples, not for an individual's gain. I rely much on my husband who supports me in my efforts. I have these questions:

1. How may we promote the kinship of women, in solidarity, without detracting from our femininity / feminine strength of purpose? In other words, how may we work together to promote a higher feminine consciousness in this world without having to detract from the work and benefit of the opposite sex (male)?
2. How can we embrace the softness, the nurturing, the exquisite nature of the female form, physique, and consciousness while still honoring the patriarchal nature of man?
3. How can we promote the sanctity of marriage and family where the feminine and the masculine meet on equal footing?
4. Praised for how we look but not for what is between our ears. how can we defeat the heavy oppression of the female form and consciousness?
5. Often not heard or dismissed as frivolous, how does the feminine find her voice in this world?

Manuel Gomez Hernandez

Born May 1885, Peru, currently 72 years old.

Though my large family lived in the mountains in poverty, to me we lived with wealth and in wealth. We had the land to provide for us—food, water, or shelter, sun. We had everything we needed to thrive including laughter. We slept outside, raised our animals, and lived as one. It was a good life. I should have been satisfied, but I wanted more. I went in search of crystals from Mother Earth. I wanted to be part of the earth, and I found many beautiful and powerful crystals. I loved the feel of them, their energies, their power, their color, and the way they responded to me. I married a lovely young girl, raised three sons and two daughters. But my wife was killed because of me when she was 39. The rich landowners came to rob us of our crystals. I needed money, so I tried to sell my crystals to them, but they didn't want to pay for them. I wasn't home to protect my family and my wife. They brutally murdered her to put fear into me. I moved my children high up into the mountains and raised them on my own. We lived a simple but good life. I knew when my wife died I had another calling—the call of healing, the call of Shaman. I was an eagle flying, and I was a serpent swimming. I knew that I was to journey in my life but never dreamed it was to another space. I always believed my journey would be into the depths of Mother Earth. I became a shaman and now understand it was always my calling. I am 72 years old now and am realizing I lived a wonderful life in spite of the hardships. I have these questions:

1. How could I have served my community and my people better in their times of need?
2. Did I learn and appreciate all of my life lessons?
3. I feel my shamanic healings didn't serve all my people. Why did I let ego intrude?

4. What did I need to release that I was afraid to see, and would this have eliminated my ego?
5. Will my children and grandchildren be happy in their lives?

Sarah Ann Benson

Born April 11, 1958, USA.

I grew up with three sisters in Kensington, Maryland. I was killed in a car accident coming back home after visiting my older sister. I had plans for my life. I was engaged to a wonderful man and was to be married in three months. I was a psychology therapist and I was building my own practice to help people in need. My life growing up was not the way it appeared to the outside world. My parents were afraid that I would say something about what was going on. I had many difficulties, as I was repeatedly raped and molested by my father. My mother knew, but I was just told to keep quiet about it. The first time, she threw me into a hot shower and told me to wash myself and keep quiet. She gave me hot chocolate afterwards and told me that was the way of life for girls as pretty as I was. My sisters went through the same thing. I didn't believe her. I have these questions:

1. What was the purpose of my life?
2. Did I help or influence others to seek treatment?
3. How could I have handled the situation I was in, in a manner that would have served my family better?
4. How could I have opened my heart to compassionately understand clients so healing would occur?
5. Did I learn my soul's lessons for this lifetime?

Breanna Alana Mckenna MacTuirc

Born late September, 900 CE in Scotland near the English border, currently 27 years old.

I never knew the exact day, but I did know I was a conceived during Beltane. My mother was a wild one and she wanted to have fun before she was forced to marry an old man. She married the old man, and I was born about nine months later. There was a question of who my father was, but as I was a girl, it didn't really matter. Lord MacTuirc could be dismissive of me because I was a girl. I don't think he was ever sure if I was his daughter or not. My mother told me I wasn't, but I did look somewhat like my father and I certainly had his personality. I grew up in wealth, but I was poor in reality. I was a slave and a pawn. I know I didn't have the mind of a girl —I was a warrior at heart, just like my father. I am 27 years old, and I feel like a little piglet who is kept pregnant to keep out of the way. I have had seven children in nine years and the pregnancies have not been easy. I have these questions:

1. What could I have done to get noticed and loved by my father?
2. Why did I let ego rule my life?
3. Will my children's lives be more fulfilling and happier than mine?
4. Can I influence my husband to choose husbands for my girls and wives for my sons with their happiness in mind versus clan support?
5. What legacy can I leave my children and grandchildren?

Thomas Drake

Birthdate: 1891, on an estate outside London, England.

As a young man in my late 20s, I went to war during World War I after experiencing a privileged life, good education, and strong family life. Adjusting to the war was difficult, and I witnessed many things that were difficult to process. Shortly before the end of the war, I was badly injured and sent back to the hospital in London where recovery took years. Even when I was released from the hospital, I suffered post-traumatic symptoms.

I lived with my sister's family and took great joy in my nieces and nephews. Funds from a family help keep me afloat. By chance I reconnected with my school sweetheart and we married. But something about this transition triggers my post-traumatic symptoms. Though we returned to my family home, our marriage was difficult.

We had two sons whom I didn't often see. I stayed married but, because I took to drink and violence, my wife and sons spent a lot of time with her family. As my sons grow, and go to university, I am left alone on my estate. Drinking heavily, I pass alone from the flu.

The timing of this reading is when Thomas is sick, more or less on his deathbed, reflecting back at his life and has these questions:

1. What does the soul gain by allowing the person to go into experiences so difficult that they're likely to die or be permanently damaged, like war?
2. What spiritual tools can help people suffering from maladies like mental illness and PTSD to see the light of hope?
3. What lessons can the soul take from broken marriages and broken families when they haven't managed to mend fences or end on a happy note? What learning can be salvaged?
4. What is the purpose of addiction in the life's path?
5. Are there such things as soulmates and why do those relationships sometimes go wrong?

Zha-Ming

Born approximately 350 BCE, in now Northeast China, currently 25 years old.

I am a stranger among my people though I live alongside them in my hut. I was married and had two children, but all three died despite my skills. I am a shaman and an herb woman. I inherited my abilities from my father's mother who raised me after my mother passed when I was three years old. My grandmother cared nothing for other's opinions and cared everything for me and that I be a woman of the stars and skies like her. Every day she taught me her lore and shared her abilities so that I could find mine. I learned to stand outside within the elements and connect single-mindedly to the connection available through nature. I journeyed to the stars and learned their healing secrets and returned each time with assistance for those who were sick and in un-ease. The trouble is that humans think "good medicine" always keeps people alive. I learned from my grandmother and from the stars and skies that healing is always from the eternal soul level and doesn't always look good. In their fear and in their anger, they blamed me for not curing everyone. I was murdered in my sleep when I was 29 years old. In the stars, I saw the deed within the journey of my soul and welcomed the transition even though the act broke their souls. None of us had choice in the matter as fate guides us all. Here are my questions.

1. What is the truth of my soul within this lifetime?
2. What can I learn about connecting with the star and skies from this lifetime?
3. What is the perspective of this lifetime within the journey of my soul?
4. Why did the act of murder break their souls?
5. How did the nature of Earth support me?

6. What is the journey of my soul?

Adelaide Murray

Birthdate: 1887, born in Maine, lived in Wyoming Territory, USA.

I was part of the westward expansion and joined my parents and siblings for an ever- westward journey that dead-ended in the 1880s in Wyoming. I lived down around the Wind River range where my father had a ranch.

I was well-educated, and could sew, sing, read and do everything that was expected of a woman at the time. But my true love was being out on the land and working the ranch. These were contentious times with local tribes.

I was wrestling with the desire to build something when I met a man from San Francisco who was very taken with me. He's made a lot of money in banking and wants a wife. At the time that this reading is occurring, I am trying to make a decision between staying in Wyoming on my family property or marrying this man, Jacob, to become a society wife. I have these questions:

1. What signs and signals should a person look for when charting their path through life? How does the universe communicate with them?
2. What should a person aspire to in life - carrying on a legacy, climbing the social ladder, or something else? What's my particular path?
3. As a woman "ahead of her time," why did my soul come in to experience this incarnation?
4. What were the lessons that were occurring and that people were learning during this period in the American West?
5. What's so unique and powerful about the underlying soul and

place of Wyoming? What's significant in a larger sense about that land?

Catalina de Gaza born in Cabrillo

Birthdate: 1552, currently 17 years old.

I was sent to what is now California or Mexico, during the era of the Spanish conquistadors. I lived a very pampered life at home in Europe but was not necessarily loved or emotionally supported. My father was abusive and my mother distant. For me, the move to California was both exile from home and family, but also the possibility of a new start and perhaps an adventure. I had hoped for more but found a very difficult life here: illness, violence, primitive conditions, and ultimately death. I didn't love the man I was forced to marry and died either in childbirth or shortly thereafter (which – she should know). I have these questions:

1. What is the soul's purpose of living a life without love? What lessons can I take away about relationships with others?
2. How do the energies of different places affect our bodies, minds, and souls? How would I experience those effects during a long migration?
3. What are the consequences of inaction when witnessing violence and doing nothing or little to help?
4. How does experiencing motherhood help us grow and change?
5. What positive lessons existed from this time of expansion, when much of the focus is on the high costs.

Maria Sanchez

Born 1831 in Bolivia, currently 19 years old.

I am 19 years old. I am a servant living in simple means due to the hardships of my country, my people, and my family. I often dream of moving to a faraway place in fulfilling my dreams of the arts and expressing myself artistically through dancing, writing and other forms of artistry. Life hasn't always been easy for me. But my family has struggled more, always trying to stay above poverty. I've become quite resourceful—a survivor. Cunning at times if I need to be, to stay afloat. I am audacious and full of life as one would say. I serve various people including small hotels juggling more than one job. I have always longed for a life of possibilities where the choices are not made for me. I have these questions:

1. Why do I live such a limited life?
2. Did I make my parents proud by working and providing for myself?
3. How could I have helped my brothers more with their choices?
4. Will I ever marry, fall in-love, raise a family without my hardships now?

Sheila Russel

Born approximately 250 years ago in London, England.

In 1787, during a time of settlement in America, I came to the colonies. I am a worker, a caretaker, a cook, and a mother. But know, I am also strong. I am a farmer assisting many men, as many of us women did during this time, in harvesting our wheat and crops to survive. I came to the new world, adopted a new name, to find a new life. I came with the hope of feeling larger in the unknown territories where wealth and one's life is not as limited as it was from where I came. I was born in London surrounded by poverty and darkness, lacking options. The wealth only came to the wealthy, and the poor remained poor. I was given an opportunity to come, through my rise above my class by working for other people with money. I came here to assist those with settling in the new world. Many women received offers to come, such as myself, who were of age to work and bear children to colonize the new land. In the open vast land, you can smell the wheat in the air. The sun beams on me, the wind blows in my hair, and as hard as this life may be with our limited resources—I am free. Free to be who I am and prosper. Escapism one may call it. But to me, it is a new beginning and hope for a better life with less obstructions and limitations. I have these questions:

1. How can I best support myself in this new life?
2. What brought me here on this journey?
3. Will my husband and I live happily and grow old together?
4. Will my children prosper in ways I never could and find their happiness?
5. Will I grow old finding my place of balance here on this land?

Tilla

Born 1012 CE, northwest New Mexico, currently 29 years old.

My story opens with my sisters and my mother and I standing on the butte at sunrise. It is what you call the spring equinox, a holy day for us. A day of solemn prayer and joyful celebration. It is for us to make the transition for all of our people. To connect sun and moon and mark the eternal motion within all. We believe that this work creates the prosperity we need to live full lives in the next cycle. However, my sisters and I know from our Mother that the Great Mother has instilled within all of us the inner ability to be bountifully connected always.

On this morning, we have all fasted for several days in preparation. We have our herbs for clear sight across the cosmos, and we are connected one to the other through blood and through heart's love. My mother is excited to lead this transition and claim the promise of the new year as she has done every spring with her mother. This is the first year of her solitary leadership, as my grandmother passed in the late fall as snow came to shift us into the rites of winter.

As the sun rises, we rise hand in hand, lifting our salutation to the Mother Goddess in her light form. For the first time, a great vision overtakes me and my sisters and we are frozen. We see strange men covered in sunlight. As they move forward, our people drop dead. The valley floor is covered with death, and the strange men keep moving as if nothing can stop them. There is a loud scream which stops the vision. In a tiny heap, I realize my mother has dropped to the ground. I rush to her and she reaches for my hand saying, "Tilla, I pass you the position. It is for you to save our people. I saw this in the stars." She squeezes my hand, her eyes flutter shut, and her soul begins the journey home, leaving me in charge.

Over the next three years, I work with my sisters and the Elder's Council. We create a plan. Four springs later, all my people have gathered on the butte for the rising of the sun. As the first light sparks the horizon, we lift our hands joined as one and melt into a separate expression of Mother Earth. I have these questions:

1. Why were healing abilities passed through the mother's line within my people?
2. How did our understanding of the cosmos serve our ability to change our circumstances and avoid the men covered in sunlight?
3. What can I learn about the journey of my soul from this lifetime?
4. What can I take away in understanding from this lifetime?

5. What did I understand about connection that would be beneficial for others to learn?

Brian Goldberg

Born in 1930, USA, currently 52 years old.

I'm an entrepreneur during the rise of corporate America, when the country became a world power. I carry the burden of supporting my family but never really followed my ambition and calling as a writer. I am too afraid to take a leap. I wanted to write stories that would inspire others, bringing joy to their lives, but I didn't. Though I lovingly enjoyed my family and the life I built for us, it left me empty. These are my questions:

1. What held me back from moving forward with my writing?
2. How did this choice impact my family and children?
3. How could I have been more supportive to my wife?
4. If I followed my calling, as a writer, how would it have changed me and others who read my books?

Valera

Born in 1791 in Scotland, currently 44 years old.

I spent my entire life living in a small house overlooking mountains, valleys, and the sea beyond. My mother raised me to be self-sufficient. When I was 20, my father found me a husband. Colin was a kind man who loved me dearly. Together we helped my parents, but they both passed one winter. Since then we have lived alone, just us two. We keep each other company, working together during the day, and at night our love is joyful and rich. Each day, the valley and mountains play for us within the motions of the seasons. Occasional visitors and wayfarers bring news of the world beyond. But we see no need to venture out. Life is full and rich and all we need. In our 85th years, the winter takes us in our sleep. These are my questions.

1. How is the prosperity of the land held within the seasons?
2. How can one learn the secrets of the plants?
3. Why are there so many stars in the night sky?
4. What can I learn from this lifetime?

16

READING WITH MOTHER EARTH

I n 2001, I began my experience with Mother Earth in the Akashic Records just after the catastrophe of 9/11. Seeking solace and support at that time, my Masters, Teachers, and Loved Ones suggested I open the Akashic Records of Mother Earth for others and answer their questions about what was happening on the planet and why. The opening experience was powerful, profound, and transforming.

In this practice, you will experience opening the Akashic Records for energy which is not human. Mother Earth put herself forward as a volunteer to help you in your journey. I include her in the Workshop Circle. Through her guidance, you will also open the Akashic Records for the elements: water, fire, air, earth, and Akasha.

For each aspect, there is a full legal name to use along with a set of questions to ask. You may also add your own questions.

Unlike Biography Readings which have a biography statement, when opening the Records for Mother Earth, you open using the process and blessing that you have learned.

1. Balance between Heaven and Earth.
2. At the entryway say the blessing for Other using the correct legal name.
3. Enter the Records and have whatever experience you have — which may be similar to opening your Records or entirely different.
4. After asking the questions and recording responses, close the Records with the closing part of the process and blessing.

Mother Earth

Full Legal Name: Mother Earth and Planet Earth

1. Why am I referred to as Mother Earth?
2. Energetically what is the purpose of a planet for physical manifestation?
3. What one idea can I understand from you, Mother Earth, which will ease my experience of living on Planet Earth?
4. How does connection with Planet Earth expand my spiritual connection?
5. What is the history of the soul of Mother Earth?
6. What message does Mother Earth have for me today?

Water

Full Legal Name: Water, the Bringer of Life

1. What is water and how does it relate to the other four elements?
2. How can I experience the primordial, potential state of water?
3. Energetically how does water create and support life?

4. How is water transformative?
5. Why does water have multiple states of existence?
6. What message does water have for me today?

Fire

Full Legal Name: Fire, the Spark of Creation

1. What is fire and how does it relate to the other four elements?
2. How can I experience the primordial, potential state of fire?
3. Energetically how does fire create and support life?
4. How is fire transformative?
5. Why does fire burn physical material?
6. What message does fire have for me today?

Air

Full Legal Name: Air, the Breath of Creation

1. What is air and how does it relate to the other four elements?
2. How can I experience the primordial, potential state of air?
3. Energetically how does air act as the breath of creation?
4. How is air transformative?
5. Describe air as it moves along the energy Continuum from potential to form.
6. What message does air have for me today?

Earth

Full Legal Name: Earth, the Grounding Principle

1. What is earth and how does it relate to the other four elements?
2. How can I experience the primordial, potential state of earth?
3. Energetically how does earth act as the grounding principle?
4. How is earth transformative?
5. Describe earth as it moves along the energy Continuum from potential to form.
6. What message does earth have for me today?

Akasha

Full Legal Name: Akasha, the Supreme Organizing Principle

1. What is Akasha and how does it relate to the other four elements?
2. How can I experience the primordial, potential state of Akasha?
3. Energetically how does Akasha act as the supreme organizing principle?
4. How is Akasha transformative?
5. Describe Akasha as it moves along the energy Continuum from potential to form.
6. What message does Akasha have for me today?

17

PARTNER PRACTICE & READING EXCHANGE

Now is the time to take your practice to the next level. To do so you need people you can practice with. All practice must be within your Agreements. This means you cannot offer a Reading to someone. You must be asked.

To maintain integrity with the Agreements, at this point, you have two choices:

- Participate in a Reading Exchange or
- Complete the Clarity Protocol and begin providing Readings to those outside of the Workshop Circle.

A Reading Exchange is a formal agreement to open the Akashic Records for Others within the Workshop Circle and the Reading Exchange protocol. A Reading Exchange may be formed by two or more people for the purpose of practice and learning in the Akashic Records using the methods in this book. You may also join the Reading Exchange I maintain.

· · ·

How to Create a Reading Exchange

Reach out to people you know who are learning to open the Akashic Records using the methods in this book. Agree to set up a Reading Exchange by exchanging the email below. If the exchange will be for more than four people, choose an exchange coordinator who will assemble, maintain, and disseminate contact information for all current and incoming exchange participants.

Each person when joining the Reading Exchange sends the following new member email to each person participating in the Reading Exchange. If there is a coordinator, new members receive the group's contact information from the coordinator.

I, (state full legal name), join the Reading Exchange which includes the following members: (list names of all members).

I am available to conduct Readings by phone, or — list your forms of possible connection.

While I am a member of this exchange held within the Workshop Circle of the Akashic Records, I will only provide Akashic Record Readings to fellow members of this Exchange and only when asked. When I feel ready to provide Akashic Record Readings to those beyond the Workshop Circle, I will complete the Clarity Protocol. When I no longer desire to be a member of this Reading Exchange, I will send an email to all current members stating my intent to withdraw from the Exchange and the date of my withdrawal.

When you receive this email from a fellow Exchange participant, you send this response:

Welcome to the Reading Exchange!

I am available to conduct Readings by Phone, or — list your forms of possible connection.

As an Exchange participant, you now have all the contact information needed to create partner practice opportunities for yourself. When you would like to participate in a partner practice, follow these steps:

- Reach out to one of the participants and ASK for a Reading as part of an exchange.
- When you receive a request for exchange, assuming you have the time to do the exchange, reply by saying yes to the request for a Reading and ASK for a Reading from the other person.

This way you both have asked for a Reading, you have not offered, and you are in alignment with your Agreements.

Know that you may be a member of more than one Reading Exchange. You may also invite another to join your exchange. If you have an exchange coordinator, refer the prospective member to the coordinator. The coordinator will share contact information so that the new member can send out the new member email. If you have a change in contact information, it is your responsibility to update the members of your exchange.

The following lessons in this section include practices for you to use in a Reading Exchange.

If you are not able to participate in an exchange, you may do these practices in your Akashic Records and then proceed to complete your Clarity Protocol.

The following practices in this book may either be done with a partner or completed solely in your Akashic Records.

Please note that in a Reading Exchange, you are not required to use questions from the same lesson as the student from whom you receive an Akashic Record Reading. Nor do you need to inform your partner what practice you will be guided by.

18

INTEGRITY

I have always thought of myself as honest. When I began opening the Akashic Records for Other, I found that my sense of integrity was refined and sharpened. In life, things happen often unpredictably. Initially, I felt a compulsion to make a Reading an enjoyable experience and felt I didn't want to upset a Receiver. But one day, a question was raised which made me see something truly horrifying: the person was guilty of rape committed years ago. Both fear and judgment rushed to the forefront of my awareness and I almost said something from the judgment. But I caught myself, realizing I was close to breaching integrity. I took a deep breath, focused on the flow of energy within the person's Akashic Records, then I relayed what came forward with as much compassion as I could muster. This was an incredibly difficult moment for me. However, as I released my initial resistance and yielded to the flow, something beyond me responded to the depth of the person without judgment but did not negate the seriousness of the topic either for the person before me or for the person attacked. I said what came, and the person in the space created took responsibility for their actions and asked how they might extend reparations. In this flow, without my judgment trying to take over and block, the Akashic Records showed me the beauty of the person's soul and what could be done to lift the fog which was wrapped like a snake *around their heart and had strapped this person in a violent act. The progress of the Reading lifted the fog, helped the person seek forgiveness, and suggested a path for reparation (which for a variety of reasons did NOT include contacting the victim). This was a very serious moment for me as I learned how the limits of my judgment can yank me out of integrity if I'm not attentive, especially within the sacred space of the Akashic Records.*

In opening your Akashic Records, your primary challenge is trust.

In opening the Akashic Records for Other one of the primary challenges is integrity.

Within the deep layers of the Akashic Records, integrity is undivided wholeness without corruption. Like truth, integrity is a bit of a moving target because where integrity is for you in this moment may not be where it was for you yesterday, nor where it may be for you tomorrow. And, like truth, being open to the motion allows integrity to be experienced within the authenticity of your being and becoming.

Integrity is the way you meet truth moment by moment. Integrity allows clarity to be flexible, not blind reaction in the moment. Integrity allows flexibility to be open and align with the moment. Integrity and its flexibility support equanimity and allow resistance with any situation to be released.

Integrity can be perceived as rigidity. However, true integrity is not binding, rather it is freedom to meet the unexpected and act in alignment no matter what appears.

With integrity, accepting whatever comes with no resistance or fear is easier. Integrity tells us about the unexpected. Managing resistance or fear allows the possibility of the unexpected to expand knowing, rather than act as a block.

In a sense, integrity is a tracking system which helps you stay on track with the truth of who you are. This tracking system allows the flow of the unexpected to come into awareness.

Thus, integrity is an inner compass with a bodily sensation or a felt-sense of balance and truth. Integrity expresses in different ways for different people. Using this internal tool helps navigate back into balance regardless of what life brings.

As witness, speaker of truth, and holder of sacred space, integrity within your heart and mind is vital. All comes together in balanced authentic wholeness within the Akashic Records by claiming integrity as foundational essence.

Opening the Records for Other will help you refine your sense of integrity and what it means for you to be in integrity. There is an effect on Other when you are not in integrity. The effect may be subtle. Experience and practice are needed to see possible effects and deal with the consequences of not being in integrity. Feeling out of integrity is not necessarily dishonesty. Rather, you are feeling the need to catch up with yourself and re-align. The bottom line is to be aware of the consequences of your presence within someone else's Akashic Records.

Integrity within the Records appears within appropriate boundaries. In a Reading, you are present as witness, not a best friend or counselor. You are to speak truth and to hold space. To do more is to overstep the boundaries that you as a Reader are responsible for creating and maintaining. If you feel compelled to "do" something, then close the Records and carefully approach the Receiver as a human being without any other roles. But do not force yourself on the Receiver. Allow the Receiver the choice of how to proceed.

Within a Reading, integrity is also expressed in honest words. What you say and how you say it match. In other words, your words and tone of voice match. Additionally, the tenor and rhythm of your transmission to the Receiver reflects, as best you can, the tenor and rhythm of the Masters, Teachers, and Loved Ones of the Receiver's Akashic Records. In honesty, you are not interjecting or deleting.

Balance is a great way to assess integrity. When you feel balance, integrity is present. If you don't feel in balance, integrity is not in alignment within you. Consider that an ancient word for sin described the action of missing the mark or not getting the arrow to the target. Integrity and balance are similar. Being out of integrity is the sense that you haven't quite met the target.

In the beginning of your experience with the Akashic Records, there may be some confusion as to whether the issue is trust or integrity. The good news is that you may ask your Records to help you discern the difference. With more experience and as trust is established, you will be able to investigate integrity and adjust as you learn and grow.

Integrity will help you keep from inserting your EBFJs (expectation, blame, fear, and judgment) into someone else's Reading. Integrity will assist you in being open and compassionate, supporting you as witness for Other.

Arrange a Reading Exchange and in the Reading you receive, ask these questions:

1. How does integrity feel to me when I am in the Akashic Records?
2. When I conduct an Akashic Record Reading, how can I ensure that I am in integrity?
3. How do I feel balance within myself? Within the Akashic Records?
4. How do my EBFJs limit or obstruct my ability to be in integrity within the Akashic Records for Other?
5. What is my truth today about integrity?

19

OPENING DIALOGUE

There was a time when I thought that before I provided an Akashic Record Reading, the Receiver needed to understand the nature of the Akashic Records. In my fervent explanations, I realized the person before me was not interested in this level of detail. Her focus was on whatever brought her to ask for the Reading.

This experience made me think of the similarity between driving a car and an Akashic Record Reading. To get down the road, a driver doesn't need to understand the inner mechanics of an automobile. The driver only needs to know how to drive. In an Akashic Record Reading, the same is true. The Receiver only needs to know how the Reading will work and their responsibility.

This realization led me to greatly simplify how I begin and end a Reading. In a Reading, the Receiver is ready to get going. The Reader doesn't need to begin a Reading by showing the Receiver what's under the hood. Any needed mechanics can be explained along the way.

The Reader is in charge of the process and progress of the Reading, gently guiding the Receiver and communicating what to expect during the course of the Reading.

As you learn to provide Readings to others, think about how you open the Reading space for the Receiver. The Opening Dialogue is everything you say between *Hello* and opening the Client's Akashic Records. Simplicity is highly recommended. Saying the same words is not required. The dialogue can be a short checklist in your mind of what you know you need to cover so that the Receiver understands the sequence of events.

For example, my opening is very simple. After greeting the Receiver, I say:

I am going to open your Akashic Records. First, I will be quiet for a moment, then I will say a blessing, then after another moment of quiet, I will say the Records are open. That's when I will be ready for your questions or any issues you want to raise.

I make sure that the Receiver understands what I have said. Then I continue with the following:

While I get your Records open, please think about what you want to know and what you want to let go.

Then I open the Receiver's Akashic Records. When the Records are opened, I simply say, "Where would you like to begin?"

As I began providing Readings, I learned what was necessary for the Reading to begin: the Receiver's questions. Addressing a lack of questions is much easier before opening, rather than after the space is created. The initial part of my dialogue signals to the Receiver what I am going to do and when. My words also signal when and what the Receiver is expected to do. If she doesn't have questions, then I can instruct the Receiver and while I open her Records, she can think of questions.

The last part of the dialogue builds on the instruction for questions by suggesting the focus for the Receiver while the Reader opens the Records. Over the years, I have found that intention for a Reading can be succinctly described as *what you want to know, what you want to let go.* This is also a subtle way to say that the Reading can be more than just a mining for information. Release and healing are legitimate flows within any Reading.

Once the Records are open, I cue the Receiver for their first question. However, I found that many people want to start with something other than a question, usually an explanation of circumstances which surround the question. I adjusted my statement to be more open ended and inclusive for the intention of the Receiver. *Where do you want to begin?*

Notice, I don't say anything about getting grounded or balanced. Nor do I say anything about protecting self energetically. Neither of these are needed because of the intention of the opening process of the Akashic Records. Please do not feel compelled to add something like this in your Opening Dialogue because you will lower the energy level of the Reading.

I also don't make any suggestions about how the Receiver should enter the Records. Anything I might suggest could be judgment or limitation. The Receiver is as the Receiver is in the moment. Making any comment or suggestion will either distract the Receiver or will inhibit the Receiver within the flow of the Reading.

Remember your truth is not the Receiver's truth. Whatever you say in opening the Reading needs to create space for the Receiver's truth. Be aware of what you say or do which might limit the Receiver in any way.

To create your Opening Dialogue, follow these steps:

Part I

In your Akashic Records, ask these questions:

1. What does the Receiver need from me prior to opening his or her Akashic Records?
2. What do I need from the Receiver prior to opening his or her Akashic Records?

Part II

Arrange a Reading Exchange and in the Akashic Record Reading you receive ask the following questions:

1. What blocks me from being fully present in my life?
2. What support do I need to improve my connection with the Akashic Records?
3. What gets in my way of communicating clearly when I conduct an Akashic Record Reading?
4. Based on the information you received above, in Part I, ask 1 or 2 questions of your own to help create your Opening Dialogue.

Part III

Create Your Own Opening Dialogue:

1. Please re-read this section, paying attention to the how and why of my opening.
2. Based on the information you have received in the preceding parts of this practice, think about what you must communicate to the Receiver prior to a Reading.

3. Make a list of these items and arrange them in order of what needs to be said first to last.
4. From this list, create your Opening Dialogue. Adjust as needed.
5. Use this Dialogue in the next Reading you provide.
6. As you use your Dialogue, adjust until you feel in balance with its use.

20

RESILIENCE AND STRENGTH

When I first began opening the Akashic Records for Other, I found that Readings longer than thirty minutes wore me out. I could be in my own Akashic Records for longer. Yet in both cases I was often left with an unsettled, unbalanced feeling which didn't make sense to me. For me to continue with the Akashic Records meant I needed to do so with a healthy vital feeling. I asked my Akashic Records what I might do differently. That's when they taught me Balance Between Heaven and Earth, presented a different blessing, and shifted to using a visualization. In short, I was given a new opening process which included a different closing.

Since then, I've made a couple shifts in the process and the blessing. I have also had many conversations with my Guides about the energetics of the process – I'm the kind of person who wants to know why.

As I made this shift, I went from feeling tired after about thirty minutes to providing both more time and more Readings. At a psychic fair, I conducted 25 thirty-minute Readings in fourteen hours and went back the next day and did a repeat.

Practice certainly makes a difference. However, the shift in how I was connecting made the biggest difference. Between practice and a new process, I was developing resilience. I became stronger. As I improved on these levels, I began recognizing that the depth available within the Reading was expanding. Focus and concentration were no longer questions; they showed up in every Reading I conducted.

The next lessons speak to this experience and provide you the opportunity to look into yourself and identify what holds you back or what you can do to expand.

I'll take this moment to say: please don't change the process or the blessing in this moment. Get more practice, and experience the support embedded energetically within for you – for it was this energy which ultimately made all the difference for me and has for my students as well.

Resilience is like water off a duck. Things are said and instead of reacting, you're able to just let it slide off. Within the Akashic Records, the opposite of resilience is inflexibility.

Resilience allows a flexibility and an ability to maintain a boundary while not absorbing or being energetically diverted by the flow of the Reading. You won't be untouched, but you are able to stand in your humanity and experience empathy for the path the Receiver is experiencing. With resiliency, the experience of the Receiver doesn't stop the flow of the Reading. Resilient, you are able to observe and witness, allowing the Receiver to have whatever experience they may have.

Within your experience providing Readings, it is important to develop resiliency so that you do not carry the energy of the Receiver with you. Water rolls off a duck because the duck's feathers are oily which in turn also ensures the duck's buoyancy in the water. Resiliency does the same for you, creating a buoyance which supports the clear flow of the Akashic Records through you. Your resiliency also creates sacred space within the Reading to support the Receiver in clear awareness of whatever is rising and shifting.

To improve resiliency, look to your inner sense of flexibility. Pay attention when your ego might want to exert itself and determine what should be different. The resilient witness within you is able to give attention to the depth and breadth of the Reading whether there is pain, suffering, conflict, challenge, happiness, peace, love, or joy. Whatever path the Reading takes, you as the Reader have the flexible resiliency you need to transmit clearly and with compassion.

As resiliency builds, you will find that you can tolerate being in the Akashic Records for extended periods of time, providing a number of Readings in a day if need be.

Strength is connected to capacity as the ability to stay strong and in awe of whatever occurs within the Reading. Strength is also an issue of stamina. Practice in the Akashic Records builds strength and stamina as well as resiliency. Like any exercise, the effort of practice over time builds experience which makes you stronger and more capable. Your experience with the Akashic Records will build a path of expansion based on strength and stamina. All of the practices are geared to helping you build the needed inner spiritual and physical capacity to experience both strength and resiliency.

Together, strength and resiliency contribute to your firm foundation within the Records. Together, both build power in the Reading. Together, both contribute to the resonance of the Reading.

However, resonance and power cannot be directly achieved. To get to either within a Reading, focus first on building resiliency and strength.

To complete this practice, gather what you need, and follow these steps.

Part I

In your Akashic Records, ask these questions:

1. How does the inflexibility of my ego interfere in my life and in my Akashic Records work?

2. How can I build strength to support my Akashic Records work?

Take some time to absorb this information.

Part II

Setup a Reading Exchange. Before you receive your Reading, open your Akashic Records again and ask for 2-3 questions about resilience and strength to ask in the Reading you receive.

Part III

In the Akashic Record Reading you receive, ask the following questions:

1. How does the inflexibility of my ego interfere in my life and in my Akashic Records work?

2. How can I build strength to support my Akashic Records work?

3. Ask the 2-3 questions you received from your Records.

21

CLOSING DIALOGUE

T*here is only one way to be respectful.*

    Respect begins with you.

If you don't respect yourself, neither will the person to whom you provide an Akashic Record Reading. If you don't show yourself respect, it's also likely you won't extend honest respect to others.

When you conduct an Akashic Record Reading outside of the Workshop Circle, especially when you accept payment, time is the primary arbiter of respect.

Begin by looking to yourself first. Are you clear about when you are available? Are you clear about the length of the Reading? Do you show up on time? Are you clear about what happens if the person is late or doesn't show? Do you begin on time? Do you end on time?

When I first began providing Readings, I was good about scheduling, being clear about length, and showing up at the promised time.

I was not good about finishing on time. I'd let the established client ask that one more question, and before I'd know it, another thirty minutes had gone by. I'd get resentful and behind. I'd get irritated with myself and I'd feel taken advantage of. I explored what was happening and why. I remembered my father telling me that there was only one way to start and end a meeting on time. The answer: start on time, end on time. In other words, if there was an issue of time, that was on me.

That's when I created two specific rules: the ten-minute rule and the five-minute rule. Ten minutes is the amount of time I am happy to talk with anyone about what I do. After ten minutes, it's an appointment for which payment is due. Five minutes is when I begin to bring the Reading to a close.

At first, I thought I might be rude or selfish with these rules. I realized I had a boundary issue that firmly held demonstrated my respect for myself AND my respect for my client. Since this clarity, I am able to keep a tight schedule, meet my commitments, and enjoy each interaction. Gone is resentment toward others and disappointment in myself.

Like the Opening Dialogue, your Closing Dialogue closes the Reading. The Closing Dialogue includes the last five minutes of the Reading and what is said after the Akashic Records are closed. Again, simplicity is preferred. Gratitude, loving attention, and clarity also go a long way to finishing the time together with honor and respect. Being clear that you are closing the Reading indicates clear boundaries and keeps the sacred space clear and within integrity.

In closing a Reading, I do the following:

- In the last five minutes of the Reading, I indicate there are five minutes remaining and ask for a final question.
- When the response to the last question is complete, I tell the Receiver that I am closing the Records and then do exactly that.
- After saying the Records are closed, I thank the Receiver for the experience.

- I am clear about what they can expect from me: how I will send the recording, and how I will complete any promises made during the Reading.
- If a great deal was released during the Reading, I let the Receiver know what might occur from the shifting and that shifting might continue.

To create your Closing Dialogue, take these steps:

Part I

In your Akashic Records, ask this question:

1. How do I close the space of the Reading for Other?

Part II

Set up a Reading Exchange. In the Akashic Record Reading you receive ask the following questions:

1. How do I close the space of the Reading for Other?

2. What stuff of mine am I inadvertently bringing to the sacred space of reading the Akashic Records for Other?

3. As a witness in the Akashic Records for Other, what can I do or release, to expand my ability to be more fully attentive to Other?

4. Based on the responses in section A above, ask 1 or 2 questions of your own to create your closing dialogue.

Part III

To assemble your Closing Dialogue, take these steps:

1. Review your Opening Dialogue.

2. Review the responses you received in both practices about closing.

3. Think through what you have received and what you feel is the best way for you to close a Reading.

4. Make a list of these items and arrange them in order of what needs to be said first to last.

5. From this list, create your Closing Dialogue. Adjust as needed.

6. Write down what you will say and do.

7. Begin using your Closing Dialogue in Readings you provide.

8. As you use your Dialogue, adjust until you feel in balance with its use.

22

STATIC AND DYNAMIC

O*f all the concepts I have learned from the Akashic Records, the static and dynamic views have had the greatest impact in shifting my view and understanding of how energy can be understood from the soul's point of view and how this view affects understanding of the Akashic. Though this is certainly a review, my intention is to explore the static and dynamic within the perspective of Other.*

Dynamic understanding can take you beyond the limits of a physical-only perspective. As powerful as they are, much awareness lies beyond chakras and meridians, beyond astral and etheric. The dynamic view is the soul's point of view – and the soul connected within the boundlessness of All That is.

The linear perspective of time and space views motion as a straight line from past to present to future. This perspective is also called the static view because there is limited awareness of motion beyond physical motion within three-dimensional space and time.

In contrast, the dynamic view takes a step beyond the physical. Within the dynamic view, time and space are infinite and eternal. The dynamic view is the view of the soul, of sacred source, of the divine. Time does not run in a straight line within the dynamic view. Instead, time flows like a fountain from this moment outward in the 360° by 360° of a sphere.

Instead of a straight-line connection, in the dynamic view each present moment is connected by awareness between this moment and the next. From a linear perspective, a random or seemingly chaotic path is created as each moment flows outside a straight path.

By shifting away from a static view, the dynamic view extends awareness of the infinite and eternal motion of the universe, of All That Is. Understanding the dynamic view is the fulcrum for shifting fundamental understanding of the energy dynamics of the soul. No longer confined to the linear or the physical, the dynamic view provides an understanding of the flow of all energy from the soul's point of view and opens understanding to the unknown of All That Is.

The dynamic view opens the possibility that human knowing can take in more, beyond the three dimensions of the physical world. The dynamic view allows for connection in time and space and beyond, outside the limits of the linear. The dynamic view opens the door to experiencing life within the infinite and eternal motion of the soul and of the experience of the infinite and eternal universal flow of the divine. A dynamic view supports the integration of spiritual and physical and does not hold back, limit, or block. The dynamic view supports, opens, expands being and becoming.

Take a moment to reflect on both the static view and the dynamic view. The mind can have difficulty wrapping itself around the idea of the dynamic view. Trying to think of time nonlinearly is brain scrambling at its best. However, given the chance, your heart may be able to feel the edges of the nuances of the static and dynamic.

Within the awareness of motion is the best way to begin to

understand and feel the dynamic view. First, remember all energy is motion. In this moment, now, is the flow of energy of you within All That Is. Take a breath and then bring your awareness to where you are now. Sense or feel or become aware of any motion within you and around you, no matter how small or subtle. When you bring your attention to this moment, you have the capacity to sense or feel or become aware of the motion of energy in this moment. Awareness of motion in this moment can also come from awareness of what is not moving, stuck, or feels blocked.

Motion is life expressing, claiming intention, gathering what is needed to move to the next moment. "Whereas no motion is in the midst of doubt, certainty, and fear, and is searching for release to move again." This sentence needs clarity.

Ask yourself a question. Feel, sense, or follow the motion generated by the question. Within the static view, questions tend to turn focus toward only one direction. Here, focus is linear.

The dynamic view opens perceptions within the infinite and eternal circle of possible motion. Here, focus is diffused, allowing awareness from many directions. The static view can limit awareness to the fear of what is and what isn't. The dynamic view opens awareness to being and becoming, to the truth that is and the possibilities that can be.

Know that this is not to say that looking at the world from only the dynamic view is what's important. Rather, what is important is that you become aware of the difference between the dynamic and the static, and to understand that both exist.

With awareness of both views, you have the opportunity to choose in each moment how you look at life. Each view presents a different vision, different understanding, and different awareness. Part of the effort to move toward spiritual-physical integration comes in understanding the opportunities of the dynamic view and not being limited by the static view.

.   .   .

Arrange a Reading Exchange and in the Reading you receive ask these questions.

1. Does the motion of energy flow freely within me, or is this motion hindered in some way?
2. How is my perception limited by the static view?
3. What one thing can I shift to view life from the dynamic view?
4. What will facilitate spiritual-physical integration within me?
5. How do I access the dynamic view of my soul?
6. Create one or two questions to ask about the static and dynamic views.

23

CRAWL: FOCUS

L earning to open and work with the Akashic Records happens in three stages: crawl, walk, and run. Whether the experience is opening the Akashic Records for yourself or for Other, these three stages apply. You also go through these three stages every time you open the Akashic Records. No matter how many times you have opened them before, first you crawl, then you walk, and finally you run. With experience, you begin to forget about beginner's mind and move dangerously close to thinking you know exactly how your experience will be. By always beginning at crawl, you have a chance to open yourself to new possibilities and unknown potential each time you enter the Akashic Records.

The first stage of experience with the Akashic Records begins at a crawl. Like a newborn baby in the first weeks of life, you are pulling together everything needed to be able to grow and expand. The energy of the Akashic Records is assembling all for you to be able to trust your experience. Because you are an adult, there will always be the big temptation to skip over this step of crawling and immediately walk or run.

However, as you begin to crawl, you are developing the ability to trust on all levels of experience. This sense of trust is coming together within your awareness and within the technique you are using to open the Records - a path of trust which requires the release of self-constructed roadblocks. These roadblocks are your EBFJs—the expectation, blame, fear, and judgment which develop from the experiences of life. Additionally, beliefs and prior experience can also become obstructions.

The push to pass this stage comes from the growing awareness you have of the capacity of the Akashic Records. You want to connect and connect deeply, to experience the depth of your capacity as quickly as possible. And, you will pass judgment on yourself about what you think perfect action should be within this context. You are worried that you can't do what you think you should be doing. You are worried that you are not receiving either in a particular way or a specific type of information. This judgment and expectation get in the way not only of expansion but also slow down the first efforts of crawling.

At this stage of crawling, the primary goal is to focus on *what is*, not what you think should be, but *what is*. Your entire learning experience is bringing your attention to *what is*. Then, trusting yourself that your attention is focused appropriately and not hampered by anything within you or outside you.

This is a process of getting comfortable with where you are and *what is* within any interaction with the Akashic Records. Your adult mind will try to make this sound easy and simple to accomplish because it seems to be just a matter of paying attention. Yet, the critical part of yourself will want to convince you that experience should be something different than *what is*.

Focus is the first motion toward awareness of *what is*. As you open the Akashic Records, the Records are actually stepping you through a process of refining your attention and your capacity to expand your attention. Keeping a clear center of interest, focus makes it possible for you to connect with the unknown and the unknowable. Every time you open the Akashic Records, the energy space of the Records is helping you by refining your focus—every time, regardless of how many times you have opened them previously— every time.

Getting to the edges of your awareness and expanding your attention, this refinement of focus relies on prior experience, yet helps you step past the limits of prior experience. Like cleaning your chalk board, you are erasing anything that has been there in order to see the new appear. Further, your board is a representation of the span of your attention and focus. You begin with a smaller slate which expands over time as your focus increases. Trying to walk before crawling cheats you of this refinement process.

In this first stage, you're learning to crawl in the Records, you're learning to trust, and you're learning to bring your focus to *what is*. Meaning that you're learning to look beyond anything within your awareness that would keep you from having focus on *what is*. And the energetic connection with the Records is helping you refine and strengthen your ability to give this attention and focus to the flow.

Let's review:

Crawling helps you release barriers to trust and focus.

Focus is the ability to have attention directed to a clear center of interest. You can have focus because you trust yourself. Focus helps you identify *what is*.

Arrange a Reading Exchange and ask these questions in the Reading you receive.

1. What helps support my ability to focus within the Akashic Records?
2. What is my truth today about trusting myself?
3. What about my experience creates barriers to being aware of *what is*?
4. What is my truth today about crawling and focus within the Akashic Records?

Several days after receiving the Reading, open your Akashic Records and ask these questions again.

24

WALK: CONCENTRATION

I n this second stage you begin your journey down the deep road. Moving outside of the influence of your EBFJs, past the limits of your personal awareness and experience, you are able to give full, focused attention toward the energetic flow within the Akashic Records. Your focus is now on *what is*.

Your attention shifts to concentration and you are able to follow a single motion within the flow. While attention is being aware of the entire slate, concentration is focusing on one moment on the slate because that's where the flow is in the moment. Beyond distraction of either time or space, you are able to concentrate on the flow in the moment within the awareness of the Akashic Records.

The flow is initiated by the intention of the Receiver. No longer just standing on the beach watching the flow toward you, in this stage, you are walking into the water and becoming part of the flow. The refinement of the focus of crawling helps loosen and release any limits as you walk. Your connection with the Records continues to loosen and release what is no longer serving. You deepen your concentration so that finer nuances begin to appear with greater ease. Limits fall away.

With focus on *what is*, in this second stage, the process is releasing what makes walking difficult. You are dumping the burdens of baggage within your awareness. The limits can be of body, mind, heart, or soul and are always emerging from your idea of how things ought to be. Your experience is what helps you release. However, your experience can obstruct because experience comes from what you know. As you walk, you are trying to allow awareness to take in the unknown and the unknowable.

Walking in the Records is like a pipe cleaner cleaning out a tube, taking away the gunk that's built up over time, restricting the flow. Breaking away the crusty bits and the sludge, the cleaning allows your concentration to intensify focus on the flow in the moment. As the tacky edges of your awareness let go, the flow is able to reveal to you its depth, its nuance, and its detail. By moving past the limits of your knowing and your awareness, your concentration deepens, expanding your awareness within the unexpected depths available within the Akashic Records.

Let's review:

Walking identifies and releases the blocks to deepest concentration.

Concentration is focus on the specific single motion of the flow. The finer details and deeper layers are revealed as you move onto the deep road.

Arrange a Reading Exchange and ask these questions in the Reading you receive.

1. What roadblocks do I construct to deep concentration within the Akashic Records?
2. What can I shift to enable deeper concentration when conducting an Akashic Record Reading?
3. What is my truth today about walking and concentration within the Akashic Records?

Several days after receiving the Reading, open your Akashic Records and ask these questions again.

25

RUN: ABSORPTION

Now you have let go, grown up, and within you is a lightness which allows you to take off, to run. Focus and concentration come together to help you become absorbed. Attention to the flow allows you to sink into concentration of the flow to the point you become so absorbed that there is nothing in your awareness other than the flow of the Akashic Records.

Letting go of the limits of your awareness, trust is here. You are ready for the layers, the deeper parts of whatever is being brought forward. You are ready for the ambiguity and the perplexing contradictions, beyond the seeming rational or sensible. As you run, an unfolding occurs to help you move forward beyond the limits of mind and what you think you know. Awareness and flow are one, joined, unified, yielding the unknown, loosening the unknowable.

You can't run until you've walked and crawled. Until you run in the Akashic Records, the beautiful, complex simplicity of any situation will not reveal itself. The complexity comes because it's something that challenges beliefs and awareness in some way. Stepping past limit, you step into the simplicity of *what is*, beyond the demand that *what is* make sense. But it doesn't have to make sense because *what is* just is.

Completely absorbed, you receive entirely from the unknown, as it is fed by the unknowable. You are not questioning truth because absorption in truth is the state of being as you run. Running is absorption, the process of becoming one with the flow as the flow is no longer hampered by you. You are the flow, and on breath in and out, expressing, transmitting the flow of the Records simply as *what is*.

Whether you are opening the Records for yourself or for Other, you are following these three steps. Each opening is for you, the Reader, a process of release and expansion. Each opening takes you beyond yourself, beyond what you think you know, to step into the simplicity and complexity of *what is* in this moment.

How do you take yourself through these stages? *You* don't. Other than opening the Akashic Records, bringing your intention, and trusting yourself, there are no specific efforts for you to make. The process of working in the Records will guide you, in the moment, in alignment with your intention and highest expression, taking you into and through each step as needed. Within one opening you may visit a stage more than once as intention is stated, explored, and understood.

Don't force effort. Allow flow to move toward you quickly and easily in alignment with you and the Receiver. Just stay focused on *what is,* and the beauty of the deep road will reveal itself to you.

Let's review:

As you **run**, the pinpoint focus of your concentration completely absorbs you into the flow, revealing layers beyond experience and thought.

Absorption is engrossed focus such that nothing other than this concentrated focus is in your awareness. Trust, truth, and the deepest layers of what is, are revealing the dynamic motion of being and becoming.

Arrange a Reading Exchange and ask these questions in the Reading you receive.

1. How can I stay concentrated on *what is* when providing an Akashic Record Reading?
2. How can I move into absorption with grace and ease within the Akashic Records?
3. What is my truth today about running and concentration when providing an Akashic Record Reading?

Several days after receiving the Reading, open your Akashic Records and ask these questions again.

26

COHERENCE

W hen focus, concentration, and absorption meld together within a Reading, coherence is achieved. Greater than the sum of its parts, energetically, coherence is more than a joining of three. The dynamics of coherence can be understood by first looking at the why of the joining and then identifying the other components of this synergy.

The interaction of focus, concentration, and absorption yields balance. Or more precisely, the interaction of the three comes from an arising awareness of balance within. A bit of a chicken and egg situation as neither is first, and neither arises without the other.

Within a Reading, balance supports the motion from focus to concentration to absorption. At the same time, the experience of moving from focus to concentration to absorption enhances the awareness of balance. Because balance always is, the interaction of focus, concentration, and absorption reinforces a clear awareness of balance within an unending feedback loop.

This growing and deepening awareness of balance also reinforces another energetic motion within. Because of the significant Earth shift, humanity is experiencing motion away from physical dominance within the world order. The new motion is to live life within a balanced integration of physical and spiritual. Balance and the conscious awareness of focus, concentration, and absorption enable the conscious motion toward this deep level of integration. Opening the Akashic Records both begins and continues this process. As you have more experience, the effect expands the integration which also enhances the sense of balance within and without.

Balance and physical-spiritual integration are both supported by and assist in moving you beyond a dependence on intellectual thought. Because the motion is to take you beyond what you know into the unknown, what you know can hold you back. Instead, your ability to trust moves you into the unknown, beyond intellectual reasoning which, by definition, is limited to what you think you know. Intuition is the beginning of this process of learning to receive from the unknown and through your unconscious knowing. Balance and integration provide a firm foundation for an inner process which initially may feel like stepping off a cliff into the abyss. This is not stepping away from reason. Instead, this is stepping into a new awareness of reason and knowing supported by an expanding physical-spiritual integration.

Overall, you are moving away from the limitations of the static view. No longer held in check by a linear only perspective, you are beginning to entertain additional possibilities. You are allowing yourself to experience life within the infinite and eternal perspective.

Focus, concentration, and absorption become steps leading down a path of dynamic living. This motion is fueled by and creates more awareness of balance, physical-spiritual integration, and thought beyond the borders of the mind.

Within the context of an Akashic Record Reading, balance and integration along with focus, concentration, and absorption fuel the unified motion of coherence. Crawl, walk, run is an expression of static living which begins the path toward the synergy of coherence. A unified whole within the dynamic view, coherence is an expression of dynamic living. Within the perspective of coherence, life exist in this moment of being and becoming.

Within an Akashic Record Reading, coherence is the experience of the Reader, Receiver, and Reading becoming one within the energetic flow created by the intersection of the three. Emerging beyond thought, coherence is a balance across body, mind, heart, and soul as well as physical-spiritual integration supported on all levels. Moving from the limits of the static into the dynamics of being and becoming, coherence is not created through conscious intent. Coherence emerges from the opening within encouraged by the process of crawl, walk, and run. In the emergence, coherence draws the Reader and the Receiver into a balanced integrated space open to the unknown and the unknowable.

Arrange a Reading Exchange and ask these questions in the Reading you receive.

1. How can focus, concentration and absorption move me into an experience of coherence when I provide an Akashic Record Reading?
2. How does my intellectual mind create barriers for me in focusing on what is within an Akashic Record Reading?
3. What is my truth today about coherence when conducting an Akashic Record Reading?
4. How can I experience coherence with an Akashic Record Reading? Within my life?

Several days after receiving the Reading, open your Akashic Records and ask these questions again.

27

THRESHOLD AND BOUNDARY

L ight is a much sought-after and often-discussed object of the spiritual journey.

Chaos, the abyss, the darkness, that without light is positioned as the starting point and the place to move away from.

To the light. To understanding. To awareness.

To come into the light is to see anew, to reach a desired goal.

My experience with the Akashic Records has transformed my understanding of light by opening me to thinking of the transition of dark to light in a different way.

Instead of moving from the dark, my sense of threshold and boundary has guided me to see this as a process of learning.

Each question asked, each issue raised, is a liminal experience where I feel myself transition from not-knowing to knowing within me.

In other words, the threshold of the Akashic Records happens within my awareness as a boundary dissolves, and I feel within me an aspect once shadowed now lit from within.

To ask a question in the Akashic Records and receive a response is always an inner liminal experience. It is often subtle. Yet still a transition in which I will swear I'm standing exactly where I began but now in a new space where the unknown is now known.

Everything is energy.

Energy expresses across a continuum between potential and form.

This is a cycle of eternal ebb and flow, breath out, followed by a breath in. Between the in and out is a pause, a pause within the infinite and the eternal expression of energy. The pause is at the threshold between what is and what will be. A threshold between being and becoming. A threshold of emergence, a shift in energetic states, an awareness of motion within the pause.

Coherence brings you to this threshold, to this liminal experience beyond time and space, existing always in the present moment. The threshold pushes at your ability to move beyond static awareness, inviting you to exist within the dynamic perspective of the infinite and eternal.

Focus, concentration, and absorption bring you to the possibility of the threshold as a continual life experience. You are challenged always to live as if you are stepping into the unknown abyss. Then, you find that in the stepping you are gathering the knowing you need to understand the threshold experience and whatever follows. You step without knowing because you are open to the infinite possibility of the unknown.

The unity of experience contains the ebb and flow as well as the experience of the pause in between. Between each moment is a threshold which ignites becoming into being. Coherence is the word used to identify this unified motion which is connected across multiple awarenesses, at the present moment.

Each threshold marks a boundary between one moment and the next. Each threshold describes an experience between each energetic flow from potential to form to potential.

Within the Akashic Records, the entire process of opening and closing is a threshold experience, marked by boundaries.

The tree in your safe, comfortable place marks the first boundary. Balance between Heaven and Earth brings you to your center as the next threshold and boundary. The entryway at the end of your path is a boundary happening at a viewed threshold. The blessing provides entry at the threshold and is its own threshold of experience. Each question asked, each issue raised requires that focus, concentration, and absorption take you across the threshold of the subject, allowing you a new view and new understanding within the coherence created. With closing, each Amen indicates the return through boundary and threshold. Each boundary provides breath in and breath out to facilitate vision of the unknown. At each threshold, you let go of that which cannot be accommodated beyond. At each threshold, the becoming shifts across the liminal into new being.

You have opened yourself to the liminal, the light of awareness at the threshold. You are moving from the profane to the sacred, from the static to the dynamic, from the consciousness of focus to the integration of coherence.

A big step in experience. A subtle step in awareness. Both taken within the simplicity of this breath in and now this breath out.

Arrange a Reading Exchange and ask these questions in the Reading you receive.

1. What will help me have clear awareness at the threshold of an Akashic Record Reading?
2. What boundaries can I release to open to a deeper level of trust in myself?
3. How can I embrace the light of awareness at the threshold?
4. How can I be aware of the pause between breath in and breath out?

28

THE UNEXPECTED

J ust when you think you know how this Akashic Records stuff goes, something will happen, and the opportunity for deeper understanding opens before you. I know this from personal experience.

I connected with a new client, opened his Akashic Records, and asked as I usually do, "Where would you like to begin?" In a quiet, measured voice, he replied, "My wife died last week. Why?"

I was both startled and triggered by the question and the initial response from the Akashic Records: Nothing. There was nothing. No sense of motion. No sound. No images. Nothing.

The starkness of the question and all the related implications hit me square in my heart. I had never felt such an intense desire to be able to answer, to provide comfort, to ease pain. But those are all human desires which are mine and don't belong within the Reading. They are nothing other than my stuff.

But there was nothing. And I was caught in a real moment. A moment calling to me to be clear about why I was present, about my responsibility in the moment, and my choices in the face of this unexpected.

Quickly, I reminded myself that all that wasn't either my client's question or the Akashic Records' response – if it came – had no place at this moment within the sacred space of the Reading.

I took a deep breath, letting go of myself and whatever my desire might be in the moment including any impulse to alleviate pain. That was NOT the question. Besides, pain could just be my assumption.

Instead, I took a breath. I asked how what I was receiving, which was nothing, answered the question. The guides responded, and I tried my best to transmit their response as it came. Which essentially began, "We understand that you feel nothing where once you felt love. Know that the love will be with you always, it has only shifted appearance." They stopped. I did, too.

I heard an intake of breath followed by a ragged exhale. "Oh my God! I was so worried she was gone forever. Thank you!"

The Reading continued, and I know this client found not only solace within the darkness of circumstance but was able to release a mountain of grief and a glacier of self-condemnation. I remember the depth of the experience to this day and know that my life shifted within the experience simply because I didn't let ME get in the way.

Leave your stuff at your door before you set out for another. Doing so allows the unexpected to be gift to both Receiver and Reader.

All That Is is the ineffable transcendence which defies description of its totality. Yet, it is within All That Is that the unexpected rises. As everything, the unexpected is energy. Your life is an interaction with the energy flow of All That Is. When the unexpected shows up, you become aware of how your energy flow is intersecting or paralleling the flow of All That Is. The unexpected is simply the unknown making an appearance because you are interacting with the motion of All That Is within your intention, motion, and knowing.

You blame yourself for the unexpected. You blame, you judge, you hold yourself responsible because somehow you should have anticipated the unexpected.

But the unexpected comes from the boundlessness, that which exists beyond description, beyond understanding, out of sight within the unknown and the unknowable.

When the unexpected shows up, often the first response is resistance with the thought, "That's not what I wanted, or thought would happen." That's both resistance and judgment. The unexpected can't be predicted or pre-determined. Give yourself a break and acknowledge that even with perfect action, the unexpected could not be seen before appearing. The only aspect about the unexpected which can be known ahead of time is that its appearance will be . . . unexpected.

The unexpected will always show up no matter the depth of your learning or the distance of your journey. Instead, embrace the unexpected and allow the embrace to help you expand your understanding and enlarge your experience. The embrace moves you passed resistance, through the threshold available within the unexpected.

This moment is only understandable in this moment. The next moment can't be understood now. The next moment can only be experienced when it has become this moment. Resistance wants to hold you back and force you to see what is on the other side of the threshold before crossing. But the unexpected can only be understood by stepping fully into its flow and opening to whatever it has to provide. Embrace anticipation as a motion forward rather than a variation of resistance which holds back.

See yourself in this moment and embrace the motion of the unexpected as it moves toward you. You don't need to run after it. Instead the unexpected will find you and, in your exchange, reveal its bounty from the unknown and the unknowable. Accepting the unexpected will enrich your life and reduce unneeded stress.

Arrange a Reading Exchange and ask these questions in the Reading you receive.

1. What's the one thing you can shift that, by shifting, will make everything else easier or unnecessary?
2. How can I release stress about accepting the unexpected?
3. How is the unexpected a gift in my life?
4. Why do I expect myself to behave perfectly?

29

VULNERABILITY

I have had to learn vulnerability. I have had to learn to open my heart in spite of past experiences of trauma and pain. There have been many experiences which would make shutting myself in a deep closet seem like the wisest, protective choice. I went through a period in my life where I did just that – hide in a closet crying with fear. It was a reaction produced by severe, early trauma.

One day, I realized that despite the truth of the painful, I had a choice about how I responded. I discovered I would only repeat the past if **I** repeated the past.

Granted there were no guarantees that I would remain out of harm, but that harm was more likely if I acted as if it would show up. I realized that the key to vulnerability was to be clear about what I could or couldn't control. I can't control others. I can make choices for myself. I can't control aspects of events that aren't mine. I can trust myself to respond the best I can in the moment, learning what I might need for the next moment. Even as an authority in the Akashic Records, I am not required in any way to predict the future. Instead, in vulnerability I am open to receiving from the unknown what I need in the *moment to make a choice for the next moment, the next step, the next opportunity of being and becoming.*

Without vulnerability, I am hollow, lifeless, and reactionary. Life is nothing but fear.

Within vulnerability, the hollow pit of fear in my stomach may still rear its ugly head. But I don't react. I lean into what I don't know, and I learn. I laugh. I love myself and all the amazing people of this world.

In vulnerability, the best of me is set free to live fully my best life with grace and ease.

The one thing certain about life is that it is uncertain. Life is unpredictable, moving toward you from the unknown.

Balanced against this uncertainty is the intrinsic, deeply human need to know, to be certain. In each moment, uncertainty pushes at this need, pushes at the edges to unravel the mystery of the universe and to know with certainty.

Much about life shows in how you decide to deal with the unknown. Are you dependent on outside sources to take a step, make a decision, or feel confident? Do you reach outside of yourself to have someone tell you truth so that you know?

When you are afraid of the unknown and lacking in self-confidence, looking outside of your heart and your awareness is a typical response. In this perspective, you want to avoid uncertainty as much as possible. When it is unavoidable, you judge yourself as incompetent and double down on the motion away from self as the way to counter uncertainty.

However, as self-trust builds, confidence in finding truth within expands. Now the approach to uncertainty is different. Instead of pulling away, you can look within for truth and for confidence that no matter what may appear, you can find a way through an unexpected challenge. Without confidence, the emphasis is perfect action, behaving perfectly. Confidence realizes that there is no one perfect response, instead there is trust to respond in the moment. You don't need to know the protocol ahead of time, because you trust yourself to understand and decide in the moment.

With this trust, rather than hold back, you can lean in and look at uncertainty without debilitating fear. Fear may still be there, but it is not robbing you of trust. And within the leaning in, expectations are different. Without trust, you are in judgment, pulling away from center, expecting self to fail no matter the circumstances. It's this expectation of failure which fuels the withdrawal. In contrast, with confidence, expectation is not present because there is trust and fear is not controlling your response.

Vulnerability can be seen as a weakness when trust is absent, and life is riddled with reaction to expectation. Fear pushes and controls and holds the heart captive to create a sense of safety.

With trust and confidence, vulnerability is the opportunity to learn and grow within the challenge of uncertainty. Gone is the demand for perfection, and the focus is on the process of engaging with life rather than a demand to predict with certainty the future.

Vulnerability is the energy of the present moment open to the possibilities within the unexpected. You lean in without fear holding you back, without worry of falling into the unknown unprotected.

Vulnerability is leaning into uncertainty without expectation.

In the Akashic Records, each opening, especially for Other, asks you to be vulnerable. The Akashic Records are of and from the unknown. Even repeating the same question will not elicit the same response — if you are open and vulnerable. The only way down the deep road is with vulnerability. There may be hesitation, mistrust, fear, or the urge to withhold. However, by leaning into the uncertainty of the Akashic

Records without expectation for either you or the Receiver, the deep road of truth, trust, and worthiness flows to you, opening the way and guiding forward regardless of response or reaction.

Vulnerability moves forward in truth and in trust into the depth of self and the now revealing mysteries of the universe.

Gather what you need, open your Akashic Records, and ask these questions.

1. What pulls me out of my inner truth to search for truth outside myself?
2. Energetically, how can I understand vulnerability in my life?
3. What fears do I have about the unexpected or the unknown?
4. How can I lean into uncertainty within the Akashic Records? Within my life?

Arrange an Exchange; ask these same questions in the Reading you receive. Compare responses, and then open your Akashic Records and ask this question:

- How can I lean into uncertainty without expectation?

30

LABELS

My most difficult challenge in the Akashic Records has been my own mind and thinking "I know." I'm smart, thoughtful, and intuitive. But when I get stuck in what I think I know, the Reading I provide suffers. It's flat, limited, and .... blah.

On the reverse, the most exciting, powerful, meaningful work has come when I get out of my way and approach the Reading as a blank slate and without static labels. I quit thinking "I know" because experience has shown I hadn't a clue. The possibility of an Akashic Record Reading comes from the unknown. If I am stuck in my known, then that possibility has no clear entry into the Reading.

The simplest way I can put this learning: Don't do labels. Don't assume you know.

It doesn't matter how thoughtful, intuitive, or smart you are, you don't know. The good news is that to conduct a quality Akashic Record Reading, you don't need to know.

Don't do labels. Don't assume you know.

. . .

When everything is energy which flows across the continuum from potential to form, knowing spans the entirety of the flow. At form is the known. As energy moves toward potential, knowing flows into the unknown first and, at the far end of the continuum, ebbs into the unknowable.

No matter the topic, knowing spans this motion from known to unknown to unknowable.

The known is easy to identify and name because within knowing the known is seen and understood. In fact, that's a good definition of known: that which is seen and understood within the flow of knowing.

The unknowable, the potential end of the continuum, is that which is impossible to see or to understand. Again, a definition. The limited view gives rise to many labels such as chaos, mystery, void, or abyss.

In between is the unknown, the flow between, the bridge through, the path across, the fulcrum within the process of knowing.

More than anything, knowing is process. Knowing is not a thing or an item. Knowing is a gathering, an engagement, an interaction, a revealing.

Yet, sometimes the definitions and labels applied to facilitate knowing, the known, unknown, and unknowable are solidified, frozen, held back and prevent understanding being achieved. The frozen moment doesn't move forward within the inevitable expansion of this moment flowing into the next. Frozen, awareness is stuck in what was, is separated from *what is*, and is prevented from witnessing what can become.

Words as labels, stuck in time, are not able to facilitate a connection between what is and what is becoming. Words held rigidly in *what was* create barriers to new truth in the next moment.

The solution is not avoiding words as labels. Labels can help in a moment of welcoming the unknown. But when a label is clutched as a brake on motion and new understanding, the flow of knowing is diminished.

Ego, soul, love, peace, pain, anger, karma, truth, friend, enemy, soulmate, and purpose are all beautiful words attempting to convey depth and breadth of experience and understanding. These are also labels which can hold you back from learning and growing simply because you think you know exactly what they are in this moment.

When release allows new vistas of understanding to move forward, the expansion that is possible is breathtaking. Awareness moves from the known into the unknown.

When you look for what you expect, all that will be seen is the contents of your mind. However, moving beyond assumption into the openness of the unknown is the bridge between complacency and deep inner growth. This forward motion, experienced freely, moves experience and awareness into deeper concert with the edges of the unknown melting into the unknowable. At this edge, the unknowable is loosening the impossible and beginning to reveal itself as knowable. Openness to move beyond what is known brings the light of awareness to that which appears dark simply because a moment before it was identified as unknowable.

Understand that these labels — known, unknown, and unknowable — provide a bridge to see knowing in a different light. In this new light, self-awareness shifts and you can release dependence that labels be unmoving.

In this understanding comes the new awareness that motion is life. To learn is a choice to engage in the motion, not in fear, but in the joy and excitement of discovery.

Spanning the continuum of energy and knowing, the Akashic Records are an excellent source for learning and questioning what was learned yesterday for new motion and new direction today.

As an Akashic Record Reader, your journey is a motion into whatever is beyond this moment. Don't assume you know what will be revealed. Ask the question, and let the flow bring to you from beyond your known, the unknown and the unknowable.

The only way for a Reading to be presented beyond the limits of personal mind and personal labels is to step forward as a witness without preconceived notions and expectations. To be open to receiving the Receiver's truth requires that the Reader step beyond the limits of label and hesitancy of mind to receive from beyond.

A quality Akashic Record Reading comes forward from the unknown and the unknowable. Held within the sacred space that you, as witness, hold despite any hesitancy with the unknown, speak the truth of the flow.

As the unknowable begins its release, it is in the unknown that the magic of a Reading begins. Connected with the truth of the moment, beyond what you know will emerge, is the beautiful power the Receiver needs in this moment. The deep road emerges from the heart of truth and knowing for the Receiver which always is beyond what the Reader knows.

Part I

Arrange a Reading Exchange and ask these questions in the Reading you receive.

1. What fear do I have about not knowing?
2. How do I hold myself "to know" within the situations of my life?
3. What can I release to be willing to receive the unknown in an Akashic Record Reading?
4. What labels get in my way within the Akashic Records? Within my life?

Part II

Pick a label word and ask these questions in your Akashic Records about *this* label.

1. What is this?
2. Energetically, how can I understand this at the dynamic level?
3. Do I have a personal block to understanding the deep road of this?
4. What is my truth today about this?

31

RESISTANCE

All That Is holds two arenas of energetic experience, Non-Physical Reality and Physical Reality. Non-Physical Reality is 100% potential and capable of consciousness but not physical form. Only Physical Reality contains physical form—from the subtlest, such as light (photons), to the densest of physical matter.

Resistance is the universal motion which assists the flow of potential to take form. Though looking from a static point of view, resistance is a stepping back, a withholding, a refusal to accept what is proffered. Perceived to have an object in the sense that you are in resistance to something, resistance is also the attempt to exclude from experience.

Dynamically, resistance is differentiation. All That Is has many levels of experience along the continuum from the ONE divine source, to the many, and to the individual one. The individual one is the experience of an individual soul, *I am*. In the initial moments of the soul, the individual's ability to recognize *I am* differentiates self from other individuals. As the many, individual souls recognize they are not alone. There are moments of experience which are more than a group of individuals but as a collective infinitely and eternally connected. The ONE source is the ineffable, unified totality of All That Is, and thus there is no energetic differentiation at that end of the continuum.

The one and the many can have awareness of the existence of the ONE. Complete awareness of the totality of the ONE is not possible because the ONE resides within the undifferentiated of the unknowable.

Within the dynamic view, resistance isn't holding back. Rather, dynamically, resistance is standing firm in a place where you are aware of yourself and you are aware of what is not you. As you begin to feel into this perspective, you will see that what is being differentiated is intention. Intention gives direction to motion. In each moment, intention is refining and shifting, altering motion. Standing firm is being conscious of your intention and in whatever manner it might be shifting in the moment.

Think of a river, water flowing across a riverbed. Which makes the river? The water as it flows? Or the channel which holds the flow?

Think of how the river flow is different from the channel. Think of a stone in the center of the flow. A flow which is pushing and pulling. Sometimes, the stone holds firm, content to experience the flow from a fixed position. Other times, the stone lets go and flows with the river, stepping beyond, looking for new experience, new understanding, new intention. Yet the motion comes from inner awareness and personal choice, reducing the sense of being tossed about.

The dynamic view is not better than the static view. At this level of study, learning comes in acknowledging that there are always different points of view available in any situation. The block of resistance comes in the judgment of one over the other.

Know thyself! In the moment, choose the perspective which helps you loosen the ties which bind. Sometimes standing firm, looking beyond the static is the best choice. Sometimes going with the flow is what loosens the stale, the old, and the no longer useful. Either way is to realize resistance is a friendly nudge of changing intentions rather than an indication of personal failure or misdirection.

Gather what you need and complete the following questions as directed.

Part I

Open your Akashic Records and ask these questions:

1. What do I need to understand to be able to see resistance as differentiation?
2. How can I know when it is time to stand firm and when it is time to go with the flow?
3. What are two questions for me to ask about resistance?

Part II

Set up a Reading Exchange and in the Reading you receive, ask these questions:

1. What is my truth today about resistance?
2. Ask the questions suggested in Part I above.

32

THE UNANSWERABLE QUESTION

In providing an Akashic Record Reading to Other, there are almost no limits to what can be addressed. The limit is that the issue raised must be one which can only come from the Receiver's Records. For example, life purpose of the Receiver is appropriate but not the life purpose of someone else. The scope and purpose of a relationship can be questioned, but personal information needs to come from the Records of the person in question.

However, there is one question which cannot be answered within the Akashic Records.

The unasked question.

If the Receiver doesn't ask the question, then there is no way to respond and remain in integrity with the process of the Akashic Record Reading.

Just as you must wait to be asked to provide a Reading, it is not your job to ask questions, or suggest questions. Asking unasked questions is rude interference, thoughtless presumption, and not done—ever.

For example, in the Reading suppose you notice that the Receiver is sad, but none of the questions raised refer to this sadness. You must not ask the Akashic Records on behalf of the Receiver. You must not comment or question the Receiver. You observe, you witness, and the only questions brought to the Akashic Record Reading are the questions raised by the Receiver.

Keep in mind it is appropriate to ask the Records questions of technique. For example, if the Receiver is not understanding a response, asking the Records to re-phrase is a question of technique aimed toward facilitating the Reading to the benefit of the Receiver.

However, to take another step and ask substantive questions on behalf of the Receiver is presumptuous and against the Agreements.

Leave the unasked question alone. Often, it is eventually asked. But until then ... don't.

Arrange a Reading Exchange and ask these questions in the Reading you receive.

1. How and why do I assume I know what is best for the Receiver?
2. How do my assumptions interfere with an Akashic Record Reading?
3. How may I release interfering assumptions or expectations?
4. What else may I understand today about the unanswerable question?

33

RESISTANCE, PART TWO

P*erhaps you have noticed that this book is not filled with account after account of the various experiences I have had providing Akashic Records Readings for Other. There are many good reasons for this.*

One: Confidentiality. *I promise confidentiality and make this commitment with extreme seriousness. In fact, all accounts in this book are either pieced together or shifted in some way that make the experience unrecognizable to the client.*

Two: Diversity. *I've received nearly any question you could think of – and then some. Additionally, I don't want the re-counting of my experience to imply limits other than the ethical boundaries described by the Agreements. I want your experience to be diverse as well.*

Three: Not a competition. *My experience is mine; yours is yours. We are not learning about the Akashic Records to compete. We are learning, exploring, and sharing.*

Four: Empowerment. *I impart all within the intention of supporting you to explore and go beyond your limitations. This means you first need to be* *capable of figuring out your limitations, and then finding a way through and beyond.*

Five: Self. *Through all my experience, what I've learned is that I am my number one challenge, block, and obstruction in working with the Akashic Records. When I can get out of my way, the Reading I provide to Other is unmeasurably better. Off-the-charts amazing. But only when and if. Otherwise, there is distraction, misalignment, imbalance, frustration. Me caught up in judging myself for being less than perfect.*

Six: Experience and the Unexpected. *I've said this before, but it is incredibly important: the magic, the je-ne-sais-quoi, the mystery, the blessed, the transcendent in an Akashic Record Reading comes in the unexpected. The subtle nuance which reveals the lodestone, the foundational shift, the extraordinary become manifest. Always in the unexpected. Always.*

This is why you cannot, should not, must not allow yourself to ask questions on behalf of the Receiver. To do so blocks the unexpected. To think you know better than the Akashic Records or the Receiver is an expression of the inflexibility and fear of your ego.

Believe me – I know this from personal experience, my own arrogance.

You conduct twenty Akashic Record Readings, or fifty or a hundred, or a thousand – the number is immaterial. The point is because of your experience you think, "I KNOW because, with all this experience, now I'm so good at this Akashic Records stuff. I'm done learning. Time to share because I KNOW!"

Yes! It's true. There are many things you know and know well.

But here's what you can NEVER know: the next moment of highest and deepest expression of the Receiver. No matter the number of Readings you have provided.

Yes, the Receiver has come asking about this highest and deepest in some form or another. Yes, you have some experience with this, but your experience is limited to you and not to Other.

But the responsibility for deciding what the expression will be is for the Receiver – Not You! Not ever. And the guidance toward this expression comes solely from the Akashic Records for the Receiver.

What will happen as you conduct more Readings is expanded awareness of the Receiver and what the person may or may not be able to be aware of for themselves.

Please resist any temptation you may have to ask for the Receiver or tell the Receiver what you think they can't see or understand. Your asking interrupts the flow and deflects the moment of transcendent awareness available to the Receiver, regardless of what they have or haven't asked.

Also, please resist any temptation to deliver advice, opinion, or solution that comes from you and not the Akashic Records. Again, this interrupts the flow and transfers the focal point of the Reading from the Receiver, where it should be, to you.

And if you are tempted, then know you are being given a moment to learn of the limits of your ego, your inflexibility, and your arrogance.

Your Perspective

As change and shift approach, resistance within builds and tightens. This resistance is like a brick wall of defiance and denial. Behind the wall is the voice of truth which has reasonable, sometimes pointed, questions to ask about the approaching shift.

Think about being aware of shift and be aware of the tightening which builds. In the tight space is the resistance and the brick wall within your Akashic Records. To get to the questions which naturally arise in this moment, don't resist the tightening or the resistance. Instead invite both in, opening to the awareness provided, and witnessing its motion toward you. Ask:

What is this resistance about?

What does this sense of movement, or non-movement, have for me in this moment?

Then follow with this question:

In the face of this shift, what questions does the wisdom of my body and soul present?

Understand that this may be a process to repeat, as each set of questions asked may bring forward more tightening or resistance.

The motion of shift can have a freezing effect on awareness. However, the wisdom of body and soul, while perhaps quieted, is not ever completely silenced. The opportunity is to utilize resistance as a source or conduit to this wisdom rather than being blocked by its appearance.

Resistance shows not to deter but to point awareness in the direction of new balance. Embracing resistance allows the new flow to emerge through a process of growing and learning rather than through an approach of more struggle, denial, or defeat. The suggested questions fuel the embrace.

For Other

In opening the Akashic Records for Other, the Reader's job is not to push into the Receiver's resistance. You may be aware of resistance, especially in the form of the unasked questions behind the Receiver's wall. This is not for you to point out. Now is time for empathy and compassion as a witness. Now is the time to allow the Akashic Records to bring forward from the unknown and the unknowable.

Ultimately, leaving resistance and the unasked, untouched is a matter of trust. Trust of yourself. Trust of Other. Trust of the flow or non-flow in the moment. Trust that in this present moment is the truth.

Awareness of the unasked question of Other gives the Reader the opportunity to observe the energetics of the unasked. Knowledge gained can assist the Reader to become aware of their own unasked within.

The unasked is not bad. Rather, the unasked is opportunity to perceive differently, to go deeper, beyond outdated belief and expectation. The unasked question lies within opportunity as a key or passageway to a new approach or possibility. Instead of reacting or denying, feel into awareness and allow the flow of the Reading to unfold from the Receiver. The Akashic Records are aware of the unspoken and the unasked as well as resistance and denial.

An Akashic Record Reading happens within a moment in time but is also held within the much larger context of the Receiver's current life and the soul's experience of the infinite and the eternal.

If you meet resistance within yourself, even when conducting a Reading to another, use the above suggested questions to harvest new understanding. Trust that the Receiver will gain awareness within the flow of the body, mind, heart, and soul.

Gather what you need and complete the following questions as directed.

Part I

Think of an issue with which you feel resistance or an unwillingness for closer examination. Ask in your Akashic Records these questions about this issue:

1. What is the resistance about?

2. What does this sense of movement or non-movement have for me in this moment?

3. In the face of this shift, what questions does the wisdom of my body and soul present?

.   .   .

Part II

Arrange a Reading Exchange and ask the same questions again regarding the same issue. Also ask the questions suggested from question 3 above.

34

DIVINE TIMING

W hen I first began providing Akashic Record Readings to Others, I went through periods when I questioned everything which came out of my mouth. Was that the right word? Does that phrase make sense? Am I getting everything out? Critical Cheryl was debating with Reader Cheryl on every word, the tone, the rhythm, everything.

I was exhausted and annoyed.

Then Fear Cheryl would kick in. What if I've said the wrong thing? What if the Receiver is harmed because of what I said? Or didn't say? What if they die because of the Reading? What if the world ends, will it be my fault?

I was holding myself responsible for everything.

I wasn't in trust. I held myself incapable.

Then, one day it hit me: the unknown is ... well ... unknown. The Akashic Records emerge always from the unknown. Which means in the moment of any Reading, I don't know, I can't know the unknown. There's no yardstick to measure whether I was saying exactly the right thing.

All I have is my ability to trust myself to transmit the flow of the Akashic Records as accurately as I experience them.

My EBFJs were nothing more than blocks to trust.

To provide a quality Akashic Record Reading, I trust. Trust myself. Trust the Receiver. Trust the Akashic Records. Trust.

Done this way, now I trust what I say within a Reading. Instead of trying to push through with the brakes on, now I am able to take in the question and, on exhale, transmit what comes without feeling the need to doubt or worry.

All of this is to say that when you trust, when you allow awareness of the subtle motions, when you are in flow, the deep road opens and the unexpected, the power and the beauty of the unknown, and the transcendent energy of the Receiver's Akashic Records flow into the awareness of the Receiver.

Trust comes in deeply learning you are not in charge. In the release and the allowance, the Reading can be provided within the ineffable of Divine Timing.

Awareness within All That Is is infinite and eternal. The flow and awareness of All That Is are one and the same.

The Eternal Now is where awareness exists dynamically.

The Eternal Return is the perpetual motion toward the Eternal Now. moves from the Eternal Now will always return.

This is the energetic basis for ebb and flow, breath in and breath out. All energy experiences the Eternal Now.

This is also how the Eternal Now is both creative and replenished.

Divine timing is this dance of the Eternal Now with the Eternal Return.

Time within the static view is the ticking of a clock, passing in a linear progression, along a time- line of events ordered from past to present to future. Time is linear, held within three-dimensional space, and nothing more.

Because the divine is of the infinite and the eternal, divine timing is best understood from the dynamic view.

To move into a dynamic view of timing, there are two questions to ask:

What is time outside of the linear or static view?

Time outside of a linear perspective focuses on motion within awareness rather than motion within the limits of physical space. Non-linear time, beyond the motion of matter, is awareness of the boundlessness—which, by definition, is non-linear, without boundaries.

What is space outside of the linear or static view?

Space outside of the linear is simply awareness, consciousness, knowing—the process of gathering what you know. Space in the static view is the accumulation of energy to create form. Without linear time, space outside of the linear is without form and is simply the expression of knowing.

Thus, in its divine aspect, timing is both awareness and awareness of motion. Timing identifies the flow or the give and take of the Eternal Now and the Eternal Return.

In a static view, time draws you outside of this moment to focus on some linear point, separated from this moment. Whereas, within the dynamic view, awareness is of the creative, divine aspect contained in this moment. Time statically pushes awareness outside. Dynamically, timing flows within the inner focus of this present moment of awareness without the limits of three-dimensional space.

Thus, divine timing is awareness of balance and truth of *what is* in this moment, the Eternal Now. What moves, returns. What moves is Now. This is timing within divine expression.

When the soul emerges from pure potential, the expression of truth is so clear, so pure, so right, light shines in and through the soul, and the soul experiences a moment of divine timing. In other words, divine timing is the soul's realization of truth within the pure potential of All That Is, an integrative moment of spiritual and physical with Universal Life Force - a moment of awareness of profound balance all along the energy spectrum of the soul. Divine timing is awareness of this balance, truth, trust, power, expression, creation, and knowing. All come together to allow awareness of the profound connection that exists within all.

Divine timing happens in every moment. As awareness of dynamic motion expands, you can begin to be aware of this eternal motion of timing now, eternally returning in all moments now.

Part I

In your Akashic Records, ask these questions:

1. What is time outside the linear, static view?
2. What is space outside the linear, static view?
3. Is it possible to feel divine timing in each moment?

Part II

Arrange a Reading Exchange and ask these questions in the Reading you receive.

1. What can I release to feel the flow of divine timing in the moment?
2. What interferes with my sense of balance and truth in this moment?
3. What will connect me with my feeling of connection in each moment?
4. How can I have my life function in alignment with divine timing?

35

RESONANCE

E verything is energy.

All energy is motion, intention, and knowing.

When a bell rings or a drum sounds the energy of the sound created moves outward to be received. Not only is there sound, there is also motion which can be felt within the chest and the rest of the body. The motion can make you feel as if the sound is happening within.

This motion creates resonance, invoking an inner awareness of the motion. Resonance reverberates within and is felt through body, mind, heart, and soul. In motion, resonance aligns with the inner essence of truth. Resonance expresses the soul's perspective of energetic motion within and without.

From the physical point of view, the motion of energy is described as vibration. Thus, vibration is a physical expression within Physical Reality. Statically, vibration is used as a measure or standard to be achieved. High vibration is equated with advanced spirituality; while low vibration indicates little spiritual advancement. Used this way, vibration creates a standard to be achieved.

Held as measure, vibration becomes judgment. Especially when interaction with others is based on the perception of someone's vibratory state. This is a judgment which holds energy frozen in the moment.

Resonance is of the dynamic view and is without measurement or judgment. Resonance is an experience of the motion of energy felt within. Resonance is the feeling of alignment, an awareness of balance in and between.

Another way of describing resonance is sympathetic congruence which acknowledges a harmony between flows of energy. In resonance and congruity, you feel how another flow of energy is in harmony with your flow of energy.

Think back to the bell and the drum. When there is resonance with the ringing of the bell, you are recognizing the alignment and harmony within. Not every bell or drum will resonate with you. Nor should there be that expectation. In the moment is resonance or not. Not as judgment but as simple awareness.

The unexpected is connected with resonance. In the motion forward of the unexpected, you can find harmony, balance, and alignment because it evokes within the essence of truth of being and becoming.

The appearance of the unexpected is not always pleasant. The unexpected can be jolting and upsetting as it pushes at awareness and reaction. Looking at the unexpected as simply the unknown making an appearance gives the opportunity to step out of reaction, to move away from the knee-jerk decision of irrelevancy.

This creates a space to reflect and evaluate what is being presented. In the space may be resonance and the ability to understand a new aspect of inner truth. Or, perhaps, the unexpected showed because of the process of consideration you engage in, if you decide that whatever is being presented does not align with your inner sense of truth.

If nothing else, the point is to step out of judgment and evaluate what works, what doesn't, and what, if anything, you need to do in the moment. You give yourself a chance to really look at *what is* and how there might be understanding in the moment, and then how that understanding might resonate.

Now, given this opportunity to reflect and become aware, the next step can come from choice instead reaction.

In this moment:

Deep breath.

Look at *what is*.

Look at your inner awareness of alignment.

Observe what resonates.

Arrange a Reading Exchange and ask these questions in the Reading you receive.

1. How do I hold vibration as judgment?
2. Do I trust the feelings of my heart and body?
3. How can I feel harmony with a flow of energy?
4. How can I feel resonance?

36

PERFECT ACTION

Commonly, linear awareness holds the belief that within any moment there is only one "right" answer. Stuck in a linear awareness, self-judgment demands perfection in all areas of life. Statically, truth has only one form which, if one is perfect in action and thought, can be discovered and utilized to fuel more perfect action. Life becomes a constant push fueled by assumptions of perfect action.

The power and opportunity of the present moment is first a doorway at the threshold to the dynamic view. From this view is the awareness that in any moment is unlimited possibility rather than one right, perfect answer. This possibility presents various opportunity and through discernment and trust you decide your next step.

Within opening the Akashic Records for Other, this idea of perfect action leads to the belief that you must always convey the *right* answer. The demand for perfection denies that anything more than the *right* answer is the objective of any Reading. Armed with this belief you have now accepted responsibility for the Receiver and their experience and have charged yourself with the impossible.

The Reader's responsibility is not to provide what the Receiver thinks she wants. The Reader's responsibility is to transmit the flow from the Receiver's Akashic Records as witness free of expectation or judgment. The Reader isn't limited by the Receiver. The Reader conducts within the infinite eternal possibility inherent within the Receiver and his Akashic Records.

Yes, it would be simpler to be charged with delivering the "right" answer. But this would mean that the Reader and Receiver will be trapped in the known and never experience and receive from the unknown. By letting go of judgment and moving beyond the Receiver's demand to know, the Reader takes the Reading into a much more powerful space of possibility and knowing.

However, as in any Reading, the Receiver has choice in how to respond to the flow of the Reading. Those open to growth and learning will be excited to embrace the unknown and use this awareness to activate new motions in their lives.

Arrange a Reading Exchange and ask these questions in the Reading you receive.

1. How do I get stuck trying to find the right answer within the Akashic Records?
2. How does my sense of unworthiness keep me stuck in the search for perfect action?
3. What is my basic fear which fuels my perfectionism?
4. How can I joyfully embrace the unknown within an Akashic Record Reading?

SECTION III

PROTOCOL FOR OPENING
FOR NON-HUMAN ENERGY

Maintaining integrity within the Akashic Records is vitally important.

Integrity supports your expanding capacity and depth.

The beauty and wonder of the Akashic Records is evident when opening for energy flows other than people.

This section provides the steps to take to maintain integrity while connecting with these flows through the Akashic Records.

37

PROTOCOL FOR OPENING NON-HUMAN ENERGY

Any flow of energy has an Akashic Record which theoretically can be opened. However, when opening the Akashic Records of any energy flow, the Reader must keep the Agreements.

When opening the Akashic Records for Other, the most important Agreement is to open only when asked and to never offer.

This is very clear when a person is involved. They ask you directly, or make an appointment – somehow, they demonstrate a desire for an Akashic Record Reading through their own volition.

But what do you do with a mountain or a river or the neighbor's dog? How will you be asked? How will you maintain your Agreements with the Akashic Records in working with energy flows which are not people and can't ask?

The key is to find a way to maintain Agreements when opening the Akashic Records for something which cannot directly ask.

To begin with non-human energy, here is the primary question to ask yourself:

Is there a specific person who speaks for this non-human entity?

Let's work through this with some examples.

Your Computer – you may speak for your computer because it is yours.

The Neighbor's Dog – As owner, your neighbor may speak for their dog.

Your City – within the Akashic Records, as a citizen, you may speak for your city. However, a city doesn't have an owner in the same way as a house or a business and thus will be slightly different than the dog or the computer.

From these examples, the someone specific is most often referred to as the owner. While this may seem arbitrary, to maintain integrity with yourself and with the Akashic Records, this is an important distinction in order to maintain your Agreements.

Generally speaking, **if an object has an owner, then the owner must ask for a Reading**. If you are the owner, you may speak for whatever you own. If you don't own something, you must look to the owner to ask for a Reading.

While the issue of ownership can be clear, the problem then becomes discerning what to do if ownership can't be define or if ownership is non-existent.

The bottom line in this situation is simple: ASK.

Open your Akashic Records and ask. Ask about ownership. Ask if you have permission to open. ASK. Don't assume you know. Instead, ask your Akashic Records.

Connected with determining permission is the issue of disclosure. You have an Agreement to maintain confidentiality. Thus, any time you open the Akashic Records of a non-human entity, you have an obligation to be clear about your intention for opening and a decision about disclosure.

Most of what I present here for working in the Akashic Records with non-human energy is made with the idea of private research and study. Public disclosure requires the highest of integrity and a willingness to be entirely responsible for disclosure and any effects of the disclosure.

As we move through the possibilities of opening non-human energy, I will also be guiding you through a consideration of honesty, integrity, and ethics within the framework of the Akashic Records.

I am providing best practices gleaned from several decades of experience with the Akashic Records and this type of Akashic Record study and research. As within any spiritual practice and study, the decision of how to engage with this area of study is entirely up to you. If you choose to ignore the ethical framework which this protocol describes and endorses, that is your choice – and your responsibility for the consequences.

How you connect with non-human energy and how you disclose whatever you receive is of direct connection to your honesty, integrity, and ethics. All of which flow from harmony, balance, and integration within all of you, body, mind, heart, and soul.

May integrity and my instruction be your guide as you step into these deeper aspects of study within the Akashic Records.

Protocol for Opening for Non-Human Energy:

When the Akashic Records are to be opened for a flow of energy other than a person, the Reader must use the following protocol to make certain that permission is granted in keeping with the Agreements and that the full legal name is accurate and appropriate.

1. What energy flow do you want to open for?
2. Why? What do you want to learn? What do you plan to do with whatever you receive?
3. Does the energy flow have an owner?
4. If there is an owner, then the owner is the person to ask for a Reading. If the owner does not ask, the Akashic Records may not be opened just as is required for a person.
5. If the owner requests a Reading, a full legal name needs to be determined.
6. If the full legal name is not clear, open your Akashic Records and ask for a full legal name.
7. With permission of the owner and a full legal name, open the Akashic Records of the energy flow. The owner will ask questions.
8. If there is no clear owner, open your own Akashic Records and ask if you have permission to open the Akashic Records of the energy flow.
9. If permission is indicated in your Akashic Records, ask for the full legal name.
10. Open the Akashic Records of Other with the given full legal name.

Protocol Summary:

Determine energy flow and ownership.

Consult your Akashic Records for permission and full legal name.

Only open if the owner asks or, in the absence of an owner, only if you receive permission from your Akashic Records.

In the following lessons, I will take you through many examples to help you fully understand how to embrace this new road within Akashic Record studies.

38

OBJECT READING

For this Reading, pick an inanimate object which either has no owner or for which you are the owner. When you begin thinking of this group, you will find that there are many possibilities.

For example, roses. You could choose the rose bush in your backyard or the roses arranged in a vase on your table. Or you could choose all roses, or tea roses, or red roses. Any of these choices are appropriate for this exercise. What's necessary is to be clear in your choice because the Akashic Records of all roses is different than the Akashic Records for your rose bush.

As another example, you could choose the very large general category of exercise. You could be more specific and select walking or swimming. Again, all choices can work; determining your specific intention is required.

Review the Protocol for Opening for Non-human Energy then continue with this practice.

· · ·

Complete the object Reading following these steps:

1. Choose an inanimate object which does not have an owner or for which you are the owner.
2. Open your Akashic Records and ask for permission to open the Akashic Records of your chosen object. If permission is received, ask for the full legal name.
3. If permission is not received, choose another object.
4. Create a set of three to five questions about your chosen object.
5. Open the Akashic Records of Other as directed, ask your questions, and record the responses.

39

READING FOR LIVING STRUCTURES

The Akashic Records of your home may be open whether you are the owner or a renter because either defines legal status. Your home may be a house, an apartment, a trailer, or other living structure. If you are renting, then you open for the space you rent and not the entire building.

The full legal name is the street address plus city and state or whatever the equivalent may be where you live. In the absence of a legal address you may use geographical coordinates with your full legal name. If the living structure is mobile, you may use your full legal name plus a description of the structure. For example, Jane Brown's mobile home or John Smith's trailer.

Follow the Protocol for Opening Non-Human Energy. Use the following questions or develop your own when you open.

Here are possible questions for a home Reading.

1. What intentions supported the construction of this home?

2. Where there any incidents during construction which still affect the house or me? How can this effect be released, shifted or restructured?
3. Does the home have any suggestions to improve my vitality while living in this home?
4. Is there anything I can do to improve the vitality of this home?
5. How can the home and I work together to improve the living conditions for us both?
6. What message does my home have for me today?
7. Is there anything impeding the clear flow of energy in and around my home?
8. What can I know about the history of the home?
9. What is the history of the land believe beneath this home?
10. Are there any toxins or other disruptive energies which need to be addressed and released? How can I release these?

READING FOR ANIMALS

F or this reading, choose a general class of animals. For example, all horses or all elephants.

I am pointing you to a general class and not a specific animal. Thus, these are examples of a flow of energy without a specific owner.

Open the Akashic Records and ask if you have permission and ask for the full legal name of your chosen class. Create a set of questions to ask. Open the Akashic Records using the given full legal name.

Here are possible questions for an animal reading.

1. How did this animal develop over the last 10,000 years?
2. What does this class of animal provide to me as support or advice?
3. Why does this animal have xxx (four legs, wings, fur, scales, teeth, no teeth, etc.)?
4. How does this animal integrate with the environment?
5. What message does this animal have for me today?

ANIMAL KINGDOM

Drilling down a little more, on Earth, there are over 9 million species of animals including insects, amphibians, birds, and mammals. Animals are multi-cellular, rely on other organisms for nourishment, and most ingest food to digest it into an internal cavity. Animals reproduce sexually and are capable of rapid movement as compared to plants. Distinctive stages of development begin from fertilization and then cell division to create the animal form.

Generally, animals are divided into two groups. Vertebrates have a backbone and include reptiles, fish, amphibians, birds, and mammals. Invertebrates are without backbones and include protozoa, flatworms, annelid worms, echinoderms, mollusks, coelenterates, and the anthropods of arachnids, crustaceans, insects, and myriapods.

What is a Guardian?

Guardian energy is high-level awareness and organization with historic and energetic knowing much like a council. Each kingdom and each classification or aspect of the kingdom has guardian energy.

Within the Animal Kingdom, we will look at guardian energy for the kingdom itself and for individual phylum.

Part I

Open your Akashic Records and ask these questions:

1. What is my primary source of support within the Animal Kingdom?
2. How do I access this source within the Akashic Records?
3. How can this kingdom help me feel safe on Earth?
4. What does this source want me to know about our connection with the Animal Kingdom?

Part II

Open the Akashic Records of Mother Earth (full legal name: Mother Earth and Planet Earth) and ask the following questions:

1. What are the Guardians of the Animal Kingdom?
2. Within the Akashic Records, how do I connect with the Guardians of the Animal Kingdom? How do I connect with the Guardians of an individual classification?
3. Within the Akashic Records, how is connecting with the Guardians different from connecting with an individual species (or classification)?
4. Beyond the Akashic Records, how may I connect with the Guardians of the Animal Kingdom?
5. What message do you have for me in working with the Guardians of the Animal Kingdom?

Part III

Open the Akashic Records of the Guardians of the Animal Kingdom as directed and ask these questions:

1. What is the primary intention of the Animal Kingdom here on Earth?
2. What connection exists between the Animal Kingdom and Mother Earth/Planet Earth?
3. What is the primary nature (or intention) between the Animal Kingdom and humanity?
4. How is the Animal Kingdom connected to Earth from a galactic/universal point of view?
5. What are my primary aspects to work with within the Animal Kingdom? (Ask for at least two different classes and then an individual species within the class. For example, if the class is insects, ask for a specific insect.)
6. As I work with individual aspects of this Kingdom, what topics do I research, or questions do I ask?

Part IV

Based on your personal interests and the information you received, please choose three aspects of the Animal Kingdom to work with using these guidelines:

- At least two different classes are included. In other words, don't pick three mammals.
- At least one is something you know very little about.
- At least one you feel very close to and are excited to know more.

Develop a set of questions to ask about each aspect. At least 2 questions are specific to the individual aspect. For example, you could have 4 standard question you use for each and 2 different questions for each of the aspects. The questions help you understand about each of the following:

- Origin and intention
- Relationship with Earth and with Humanity
- Guidance, healing and balancing effects (i.e. what is their medicine?)
- Message for you
- Connections with other Kingdoms
- Color associations

The objective is to find out as much as you can about the three aspects you have chosen.

42

PLANT KINGDOM

There are approximately 400,00 plant species with 10 major divisions, of which roughly ninety percent are flowering plants. Generally, plants have low motility and manufacture their own food. Plants have a cell structure with walls containing cellulose, are multi-cellular, and are capable of photosynthesis.

Plants include trees, forbs, shrubs, grasses, vines, ferns, and mosses. Historically fungi, lichens, and bacteria were included in the Plant Kingdom, but no longer. Nor are viruses or slime molds included.

Like the Animal Kingdom there are also Guardians in the Plant Kingdom. In this practice you will explore the Guardians in the same way you explored Guardians for the Animal Kingdom.

Part I

Open your Akashic Records and ask these questions:

1. What is my primary source of support within the Plant Kingdom?
2. How do I access this source within the Akashic Records?
3. How can this kingdom help me feel safe on Earth?
4. What does this source want me to know about our connection with the Plant Kingdom?

Part II

Open the Akashic Records of Mother Earth and ask the following questions:

1. What are the Guardians of the Plant Kingdom?
2. Within the Akashic Records, how do I connect with the Guardians of the Plant Kingdom? How do I connect with the Guardians of an individual classification?
3. Within the Akashic Records, how is connecting with the Guardians different from connecting with an individual species (or form)?
4. Beyond the Akashic Records, how may I connect with the Guardians of the Plant Kingdom?
5. What message do you have for me in working with the Guardians of the Plant Kingdom?

Part III

Open the Akashic Records of the Guardians of the Plant Kingdom as directed and ask these questions:

1. What is the primary intention of the Plant Kingdom here on Earth?
2. What connection exists between the Plant Kingdom and Mother Earth/Planet Earth?
3. What is the primary nature (or intention) between the Plant Kingdom and humanity?

4. How is the Animal Kingdom connected to Earth from a galactic/universal point of view?
5. What are my primary aspects to work with within the Plant Kingdom? (Ask for at least two different phyla and then an individual species within the phylum. For example, if the phylum is no seeds, ask for a specific example.)
6. As I work with individual aspects of this Kingdom, what topics do I cover or questions do I ask?

Part IV

Based on your personal interests and the information you received, please choose three aspects of the Plant Kingdom to work with using these guidelines:

- At least two different classes are included. In other words, don't pick three seeded plants.
- At least one is something you know very little about.
- At least one you feel very close to and are excited to know more.

Develop a set of questions to ask about each aspect. At least 2 questions are specific to the individual aspect. For example, you could have 4 standard question you use for each and 2 different questions for each of the aspects. The questions help you to understand the following about each aspect:

- Origin and intention
- Relationship with Earth and with Humanity
- Guidance, healing and balancing effects (i.e., what is their medicine?)
- Message for you
- Connections with other Kingdoms
- Color or other associations

The objective is to find out as much as you can about the three aspects you have chosen.

43

MINERAL KINGDOM

The Mineral Kingdom includes minerals, gemstones, metals, and rocks whether in solid, gas, or liquid form. A mineral naturally occurs in the Earth's crust and is defined as an inorganic solid with distinct chemistry and crystalline structure. A rock is an amalgamation of two or more minerals. A gemstone is a mineral or rock, cut and polished for use. Though not all considered as gemstone are mineral. For example, amber considered a gemstone is petrified tree resin. Metals have high electrical and heat conductivity, luster, malleability, and are generally classified by their position on the Periodic Table.

Part I

Open your Akashic Records and ask these questions:

1. What is my primary source of support within the Mineral Kingdom?
2. How do I access this source within the Akashic Records?

3. How can this kingdom help me feel safe on Earth?
4. What does this source want me to know about our connection with the Mineral Kingdom?

Part II

Open the Akashic Records of Mother Earth and ask the following questions:

1. What are the Guardians of the Mineral Kingdom?
2. Within the Akashic Records, how do I connect with the Guardians of the Mineral Kingdom? How do I connect with the Guardians of an individual classification?
3. Within the Akashic Records, how is connecting with the Guardians different from connecting with an individual Mineral (or form)?
4. Beyond the Akashic Records, how may I connect with the Guardians of the Mineral Kingdom?
5. What message do you have for me in working with the Guardians of the Mineral Kingdom?

Part III

Open the Akashic Records of the Guardians of the Mineral Kingdom as directed and ask these questions:

1. What is the primary intention of the Mineral Kingdom here on Earth?
2. What connection exists between the Mineral Kingdom and Mother Earth/Planet Earth?
3. What is the primary nature (or intention) between the Mineral Kingdom and humanity?
4. How is the Mineral Kingdom connected to Earth from a galactic/universal point of view?
5. What are my primary aspects to work with within the

Mineral Kingdom? (Ask for at least two different groups and
then an individual form within the group.)

6. As I work with individual aspects of this Kingdom, what
topics do I cover or questions do I ask?

Part IV

Based on your personal interests, the information you received, and
the list of minerals by group above, please choose three aspects of the
Mineral Kingdom to work with using these guidelines:

- At least two different groups are included. In other words,
  don't pick three sulfates.
- At least one is something you know very little about.
- At least one you feel very close to and are excited to know
  more.

Develop a set of questions to ask about each aspect. At least 2
questions are specific to the individual aspect. For example, you could
have 4 standard question you use for each and 2 different questions
for each of the aspects. The questions help you to understand the
following about each aspect:

- Origin and intention
- Information about the color, shape, hardness, streak and
  luster from an energetic point of view
- Relationship with Earth and with Humanity
- Guidance, healing and balancing effects (i.e., what is their
  medicine?)
- Message for you
- Connections with other Kingdoms

The objective is to find out as much as you can about the three aspects
you have chosen.

. . .

N. B. If you have a copy of my practice book *Expand Your Practice: Ritual, Gemstones, and Aromatherapy in Your Akashic Records*, then I highly recommend that you take what you have just learned about opening for non-human energy and re-visit the process of building your own Gemstone and Aroma Dictionary. Now you can open the Akashic Records of a specific gemstone, mineral, or metal and ask for direct input. You may also work with the Guardians of gemstones and aromas in the Records to seek more specific and detailed information for yourself. If you do not have this book, send me email and request it. I will get a copy for you at no charge.

44

LANDFORMS AND FORCES

The geologic layout of Earth reflects the physical and spiritual motion of Mother Earth and Planet Earth. This motion includes both constructive and destructive weather, elemental and land movements, contraction and expansion, and multi-dimensional connections and influences.

For the purposes of this lesson, work with either general or specific forms and forces. For example, lakes and mountains are general and the Dead Sea and Mountain Everest are specific. Consider formations of earth, water, fire, or air (weather). Consider forces such as erosion, glaciers, wind, plate tectonics, volcanoes, earthquakes, wildfires, lightning, avalanches, flood, tornado, tsunami, and cosmic impact.

Part I

Open the Akashic Records of Mother Earth and Planet Earth and ask the following questions:

1. What is the history of Mother Earth?

2. What is the history of Planet Earth?
3. How are Mother Earth and Planet Earth related to Divine Source?
4. How Mother Earth – Planet Earth connected to all dimensions, known, unknown, and unknowable?
5. How is Earth connected and influenced by other physical, spiritual or universal dimensions?
6. What is motion within Mother Earth and Planet Earth?
7. How are the motions on Earth connected or influenced?
8. Why is motion both constructive and destructive?
9. What is contraction and expansion within Earth?
10. Please suggest three forms and three forces for me to utilize in the next part of the practice.

Part II

Pick three forms and three forces of Earth and ask the following questions of each within the Akashic Records of Mother Earth-Planet Earth:

1. What is the story of this form/force on Earth?
2. How is form/force related to the physical motion and to the spiritual motion of Mother Earth-Planet Earth?
3. How is the motion of form/force reflected of or connected to contraction and expansion on Earth?
4. How can I expand spiritual growth through awareness or connection with form/force?
5. Ask 1 or 2 of your own questions.

Part III

Wait a week or so and then open the Akashic Records of each of your choices in Part II. Ask the same questions from Part II. Notice any differences and if there is expansion from the first experience.

45

SACRED SITES

When I travel, I enjoy working with the Akashic Records. Visiting ancient, sacred sites is always interesting because of the strong feelings of history and connection. Opening the Akashic Records of the site adds another dimension of experience and deepens the sense of awareness about the alignment or genius of the place. This is something I do for my own support and enjoyment.

What makes a site sacred? That's often what I explore. In part it's about history and interaction, about the story which has been built over time. Often a sacred site began with a tree or a stone or another indicator of divine presence. Maybe there was an event which began acknowledgment. In some areas, I have connected to energy from the future and energy beyond Earth. In some, there is a defined presence we acknowledge as God or a form of divine expression. Sometimes a site is sacred just for you simply because it is. I have several sites that for me provide deep connection and awareness which are neither well-known or acknowledged by others.

. . .

For a general understanding about sacred sites, ask these questions in your Akashic Records.

1. What is sacred?
2. What makes a location or structure sacred?
3. What makes a site sacred for me?
4. Where does the sense of balance, connection and alignment come from within a sacred site?
5. What sacred sites on the Earth today do I find alignment and support? Why?
6. What topics or questions do I ask about sacred sites?

Select a sacred site, consult your Akashic Records for permission to open and a full legal name. Ask the following questions and add your own.

1. What is the origin of this site?
2. What is the sacred story associated from this site? Where does this story originate?
3. What imbues the sense of sacred within this location or structure?
4. Was the location considered sacred before the construction of the structure? Why?
5. Does the sense of sacred come from an alignment with Earth's energy?
6. How does alignment with Earth's energy function within this site or structure?

SECTION IV

MOVING OUTSIDE THE WORKSHOP CIRCLE

As I've said, there are many possibilities for engaging with the Akashic Records.

You may feel that continuing to explore the depths of the Akashic Records through further study is most appropriate for you at this time.

You might also want to continue to study and, also, provide Readings when asked by family and friends.

Or you might be interested in conducting Akashic Record Readings within a professional capacity.

In whatever manner you choose to move forward, you will be best served by being clear about your intention.

In this section, I help you set your intention and prepare you to move outside the Workshop Circle.

Know that this is a process you might engage in as your Akashic Records experience opens new vistas and unexpected opportunity.

Welcome! A new journey awaits!

6

CLARITY PROTOCOL

As an Akashic Record Reader, you owe it to yourself and those to whom you provide an Akashic Record Reading to be clear about how and when.

The Clarity Protocol establishes your intention with the Akashic Records and how you will proceed from this point. The Clarity Protocol helps you find your path from student to practitioner.

Before beginning the Protocol, I highly recommend successful completion of *Open the Akashic Records for Other* (this book or workshop) which I define as follows:

- Successful completion of *Open Your Akashic Records*, either book or workshop.
- Read Section I of this book and complete the personal practices within Agreements (#10), blessing (#12), and process (#13) of opening for Other.
- Accept, sign, and date the Agreements for Opening the Akashic Records for Other (Lesson 10)
- Complete at least ten Biography Readings (Lesson 15)

- Complete the Readings with Mother Earth (Lesson 16)
- Create (and re-shape as needed) an Opening and Closing Dialogue (Lessons 19 & 21)
- Complete all lessons in Section II (Lessons 18-36), preferably within at least ten Reading Exchanges. If you don't have access to a Reading Exchange, then the lessons can be completed within your Akashic Records.
- Complete all the lessons in Section III, Protocol for Opening for Non-Human Energy.
- Complete the Clarity Protocol as directed in this section.

Also please know that I describe three paths of intention and fully expect that you may choose more than one and that your final statement of intention will reflect both your interests in the Akashic Records and your unique life experience.

If at some point, you need assistance or have a question, please reach out, email me your questions and I will make every effort to help.

To give you an idea of some of the ways you might proceed, here are definitions for the three paths generally available.

Path One: Research & Study Intention

Though you may not be interested in providing Akashic Records to Others, you are interested in advanced study in the Akashic Records. You want to study more via books or workshops, you want to continue within your Akashic Records, and you may want to learn how to work in the Akashic Records of non-human energy.

Path Two: Personal Intention

You want to continue a connection with your Akashic Records and perhaps, when asked, provide Akashic Record Readings to family, friends, and acquaintances. You may accept some compensation, but you are not stepping into professional intention. You may also decide to develop a path of research and study within the Akashic Records.

Path Three: Professional Intention

Two elements distinguish professional intention: public and payment. You are publicly making yourself available for Akashic Record Readings and you will ask for monetary compensation. You will do this either by establishing a new business or by adding Akashic Record Readings as an additional service within an established business. You will also be clear about personal intention and maintain and expand your capacity as an Akashic Record Reader; you will be clear about how you will create research and study intention within the Akashic Records.

Know that whatever choices you make now can be adjusted and amended at any point in the future. Just return and step through the Protocol to re-adjust and re-direct.

The Clarity Protocol has these steps:

- Check personal progression: where are you with your connection with the Akashic Records?
- Determine intention: what are your paths within the Akashic Records?
- Client Information Sheet: what needs to be communicated about how and when you provide an Akashic Record Reading?
- Activate intention: communicate with the Akashic Records (and with me if you would like) about your intention.

The following lessons take you through these steps.

47

PROGRESSION SUMMARY

*I*n my original Akashic Records study program, the sixth month required extensive effort from the student to evaluate experience gained and to investigate opportunities available.

Before you go any further, please re-read both sets of Agreements with the Akashic Records.

Also, please look into your Akashic Records Journal and look through the work you have done. Remind yourself about where you started and where you are today.

Part I — Initial Personal Summary

Think of two or three Readings you have conducted in your studies. For each Reading answer these questions without opening your Records. After answering, create a summary for yourself and an action plan if needed.

1. From your point of view, how did the Reading you provided go?
2. What did you learn about yourself as an Akashic Record Reader from this Reading?
3. In what way did you get in the way of the flow of the Reading? What can you do to shift this?
4. How does this Reading encourage you to expand and move forward as an Akashic Record Reader?

Part II — Exploration Summary

First open your Akashic Records; ask these questions. If available, arrange two Reading Exchanges and ask these questions in the Readings you receive. Take notes during the Readings you receive.

1. As a Witness in the Akashic Records, what challenges remain before me?
2. What needs attention to improve my ability to hold sacred space for Other?
3. As a speaker of truth, what barriers to truth's clearest expression do I hold and need to release? How?
4. What has been my greatest challenge in reading for Other? What can I do about this challenge in the next six months?

Looking at your notes and your Akashic Records journal, begin with the responses of the first question. Summarize in one or two paragraphs the important points. Make a summary for the other questions. With the summaries, you have an awareness of what lies before you in your Akashic Records studies. Take steps to address anything which needs attention now.

Part III — Concluding Personal Summary

Arrange two Reading Exchanges and in the Readings you receive ask these questions. After both Readings, open your Records and ask the same questions.

1. Ask one or two questions of your choosing related to the information from either Part I or Part II above. (same questions in all Readings)
2. Am I ready to read the Akashic Records for Other outside the workshop circle? Why or why not?
3. What is my path as a Witness in the Akashic Records?

Take some time to reflect on your journey and where you'd like to go from here.

48

SETTING INTENTION

Now is the time to set aside assumptions about how you think you might move forward. Go through each part and do the work for each path.

Part I

Open your Akashic Records and ask these questions. If you would like another point of view, arrange for a Reading Exchange and ask the same questions in this order.

Path One: Research & Study Intention

Though you may not be interested in providing Akashic Records to Others, you are interested in advanced study in the Akashic Records. You want to study more via books or workshops, you want to continue within your Akashic Records, and you may want to expand your efforts in the Akashic Records of non-human energy.

- How do I continue my Akashic Records studies?
- Are there particular paths for me to explore?

Path Two: Personal Intention

You want to continue a connection with your Akashic Records and perhaps, when asked, provide Akashic Record Readings to family, friends, and acquaintances. You may accept some compensation, but you are not stepping into professional intention. You may also decide to develop a path of research and study within the Akashic Records.

- Is it part of my practice with the Akashic Records to provide Akashic Record Readings outside the Workshop Circle?
- To whom do I provide Readings?
- Do I accept compensation and in what form?

Path Three: Professional Intention

Two elements distinguish professional intention: public and payment. You are publicly making yourself available for Akashic Record Readings, and you will ask for monetary compensation. You will do this either by establishing a new business or by adding Akashic Record Readings as an additional service within an established business. You will also be clear about personal intention and maintain and expand your capacity as an Akashic Record Reader; you will be clear about how you will create research and study intention within the Akashic Records.

- Do I provide Akashic Record Readings publicly?
- What length Readings do I conduct?

- Are there special Readings to provide?
- How do I incorporate research or advanced study into my practice with the Akashic Records?
- What else do I need to know about providing Akashic Record Readings to the public?
- In what circumstances would I not charge for a Reading?
- Within professional intention, how do I work with family and friends in the Akashic Records?

Part II

Look back at your Progression Summary and the response in Part I above.

Do you have everything you need to make a decision about each form of intention?

If not, do what is necessary to feel prepared.

Now is the time to clarify your intention in the form of intention statements. Without opening your Records, complete these sentences with as much detail as is needed to be clear. If you will not declare an intention, simply write that down.

For research and study in the Akashic Records, my current intention is:

Shifts in this intention may be necessary if or when:

For personal intention with the Akashic Records, my current intention is:

Shifts in this intention may be necessary if or when:

For professional intention with the Akashic Records, my current intention is:

Shifts in this intention may be necessary if or when:

Adjust your statements in each path until you feel you have successfully described your intention.

49

CLIENT INFORMATION SHEET

E arly in my career as an Akashic Record Reader, I realized I had a bit of a problem with the expectations of those asking me for a Reading. Since much of the information about the Akashic Records was and is at best outdated, I found many people didn't understand the possibilities within a Reading. In the not knowing, some would think of me as a psychic – which isn't the full extent of possibility. While others would think of me as a therapist – which is definitely not the case both from a legal point of view as well as a practical one. An Akashic Record Reader occupies a space of extending guidance, much like a counsellor, yet from a spiritual point of view. While the experience may feel psychic to some, an Akashic Record Reader, in the way I work with the Records, is operating from a very different energy perspective than most clairvoyants.

Additionally, I realized that I needed to be clear about the terms by which I provide a Reading. I did some research into how other healing professions deal with dispensing information to new clients. My Client Information Sheet was the result of both this search and the support I received from the Akashic Records. I have coached each of my students through the process of creating this view of their work within the Records. This sheet helps both

Reader and Receiver be clear in intention and set realistic expectations on both sides.

Prior to conducting the Reading for a new client, you will share your Client Information Sheet. This sharing may be in the form of a printed page if the Reading is in person or a link to a web page for online scheduling. This sheet briefly describes the Akashic Records, defines all must-knows, and lists the terms by which you provide Readings.

Whether you are moving outside of the Workshop Circle for either professional or personal intention, you need to have your Client Information Sheet. Readers with professional intention will usually have more details than those with personal intention.

The Client Information Sheet contains two sections: definitions and administrative.

The first section is a definition, must-know section, answering in simple terms these questions:

- What are the Akashic Records?
- What elements are important for the Receiver to know about an Akashic Record Reading?

Quoting from my Client Information Sheet, the three important elements are:

Use your common sense

In our work together, whether an Akashic Record Reading, workshop or other exchange, the most important thing for you to do is use your common sense. This is not about me telling you what to do in your life. You receive from the deep knowing of your soul the information and energy you need to make your own life decisions based on what you know to be true about yourself. If something doesn't make sense, please ask for clarification. If it still doesn't make sense or it seems like something you don't agree with, know that it may make sense in the future or it is possible that the lack of clarity may be exactly what you need to help you find your best path.

Our work together is spiritual

I am neither a licensed counselor nor a physician. I provide my services and workshops in support of your spiritual development. Nothing said in a Reading, workshop, or other service should be taken as a reason or excuse to avoid appropriate medical or psychological treatment. Because I see exchange and experience with the Akashic Records as spiritual in nature, all services and workshops I provide are done as a supplement or an addition to whatever treatment or other study you are currently receiving or may seek in the future.

Commitment to confidentiality.

I will not disclose the content of your Reading to anyone (unless required by law). I will not admit to a third party that you have had an appointment with me or participate in one of my workshops or other services. If you disclose the content of your Reading or learning to a third party, you are responsible for any effects this disclosure may have. I am not responsible for your disclosure.

The second section is administrative and, depending on your intention, describes how, when, and where you provide Akashic

Record Readings. This includes pricing, how to schedule, cancellations, no-shows, refunds, and whatever else may be relevant.

For those with just personal intention, this sheet may be only one or two paragraphs. For those with professional intention, the client information sheet will contain more information and details.

Go to my website and find my Client Information page (www.cherylmarlene.com/client-information/). This will give you an idea of what I have in mind for you. Your client-information sheet doesn't have to be exactly like mine, but you may borrow freely to construct yours.

To complete this practice, gather what you need, and follow these steps.

Part I

To construct the first section, begin by writing an answer to this question: What are the Akashic Records?

In your Akashic Records, ask these questions:

1. In addition to: use your common sense, our work together is spiritual, and my commitment to confidentiality, are there additional elements of an Akashic Record Reading of which I will inform the Receiver before I provide an Akashic Record Reading?
2. What does it mean for a client to use their common sense in an Akashic Record Reading?
3. What does it mean for a client that an Akashic Record Reading is provided as spiritual support?
4. What is confidentiality in an Akashic Record Reading, and how do I maintain this level of confidentiality?
5. Ask for a definition of any other elements received in the first question.

Part II

To construct the second section, begin by asking these questions in your Akashic Records:

1. What responsibilities do I have toward my clients in providing an Akashic Record Reading?
2. What responsibilities does the Receiver have in receiving an Akashic Record Reading from me?

Make a list of administrative items which need to be covered in your client information sheet. These will include, but are not limited to, contact information, how to schedule an appointment, rates, payment, appointment types and length, cancellations, no-shows, refunds, rescheduling, and late-starts.

Part III

Put together everything that came from Part I and Part II on one page, listing the administrative details second. Edit as necessary. Decide how you will convey this to a new client before a Reading.

50

ACTIVATING YOUR CLARITY PROTOCOL

My journey in the Akashic Records has been a continuing process of intention, alignment, and balance. Clarity, while sometimes challenging, takes you a long way down your path. Now it's time to activate a new part of your journey!

Review the components of your Clarity Protocol.

- Your intention statements.
- Your Client Information Sheet.

Is anything missing or need shifting? When you are ready, continue.

Open your Akashic Records and read your intention statements and your Client Information Sheet to your Masters, Teachers, and Loved Ones. Finish with this statement:

I hereby declare my Clarity Protocol and now fully step forward with clear intention with the Akashic Records. If at some point in the future I choose to shift my intention, I will re-visit my intention statements and adjust as necessary.

Perhaps there will be a response; perhaps not. Close your Akashic Records.

In love and light, I thank you for joining me on this journey!

You are complete!

P. S. If you would like, I would be happy to receive your intention statements – just connect by email! (connect@cherylmarlene.com)

INVITATION

Now is the moment to stop, take a breath, and consider. Think about where you were when you first began this journey into the Akashic Records of Other. Think about how you felt and your concerns.

Now, think about where you are in this moment. Give yourself credit for all that you have learned, all that you have received, and all that you have opened to.

An amazing journey! I know that I was a bit overwhelmed because what I learned made me aware of the possibilities available.

That's what is before you: the possibility of the deep road. A life's journey with new destination rising always with each turn of the road.

I invite you to continue your exploration and lean into the best you are and can become. Within the Akashic Records, you can expand your journey by learning to work at deeper levels with the energies of non-human or inanimate forms. You may step into the path of deep research. You may explore advanced topics such as healing and trauma. I am here to travel with you and offer advanced study options and custom experiences.

Take another deep breath. Know, just as you are, you are ready to continue into the unknown mysteries. Your body, mind, heart, and soul are your companions as you step deeper into your becoming.

Keep in touch and let me know of your travels!

Laugh always.

Learn always.

Love always.

In Joy!

Cheryl

PS – One of the best way to stay connected with me is through my newsletter: https://www.cherylmarlene.com/newsletter/. Plus I also have this bonus practice book for you: Mother Earth and the Eternal Return – download here: https://dl.bookfunnel.com/itetfj1yyr

---

Akashic Records Master Course

Introduction to the Akashic Records

Open Your Akashic Records

Open the Akashic Records for Other

Soul Energy Dynamics and the Akashic Records

Healing in the Akashic Records

ABOUT THE AUTHOR

www.cherylmarlene.com

Cheryl Marlene is all about soul perspective, heart connection, and deep knowing.

The world's authority on the Akashic Records, she is also a mystic who is unafraid of the tough, the raw, and the real aspects of doing deep work. She conducts Readings and teaches students to access the Akashic Records through her signature *Akashic Records Master Course*.

In the field of consciousness, she is known as a futurist, innovator, and master teacher who delivers life-changing lessons with warmth and humor. Her exploration takes her to the cutting edge: bringing the future to you today, to help prepare you for what you will need tomorrow.

Cheryl's clients and students know her as a relatable, funny, everyday person who loves red dresses, urban fantasy books, and skinny margaritas. She is also an avid hiker. Her claim for herself is poetic soul, sharp mind, beautiful body, open heart.

Laugh. Learn. Love. Be. Become. Always.

Made in the USA
Las Vegas, NV
14 November 2020